Editoria

Since the last issue of *Chapman* went to the printers, three deaths have occurred which have greatly saddened the literary world: those of novelist Jessie Kesson, poet William Montgomerie and, at a tragically early age, film-maker and collector Barbara Grigor.

William Montgomerie had been ill for a long time, and reached the venerable age of 90, but his work had never quite achieved the recognition it deserved. A very scholarly man, his theories about Shakespeare were complex but will still have to be explored and evaluated. His poetry was published by Canongate some years ago, but he was seldom asked to read in public. In 1986 *Chapman 46* produced a special feature on his work, (which is still available £1.20+p&p), and gives an idea of his range as a writer. His work with his wife Nora, who survives him, on folklore and children's rhymes, is a permanently valuable contribution.

Jessie Kesson's relationship with *Chapman* goes back a long way, to *Woven by Women* 1980, where we published a review of *The White Bird Passes* and a short story, 'Morning Has Broken'. Jessie was a popular reader, and loved nothing better than to set off 'on the road', especially on a visit to give readings and workshops in her native Scotland. She is the classic example of native talent surfacing in spite of circumstances and this is more evident than in her novel and award-winning film, *Another Time Another Place*. It is especially sad that her death occurred so soon after the death of her husband, Johnnie, whose lingering terminal illness had restricted her activities. We briefly mark her death in this issue with 'It was Upon A Lammas Nicht', a short play by Jessie which was, it so happens, awaiting publication in *Chapman* when she died.

Barbara Grigor was, like Jessie, a unique spirit, always full of inspirational enthusiasm, good humour and courage. Her pioneering work with her husband Murray, especially in the field of Scottish kitsch, has enabled us to understand better our complicated and at times convuluted country. She will be greatly missed.

Ian Hamilton Finlay issue

Jonathan Hirschfeld has asked us to point out that he was not – as Angus Calder stated in his article 'The Wars of Ian Hamilton Finlay' in *Chapman* 78-9 – found guilty of slander but of disseminating selected fragments of Ian Hamilton Finlay's correspondence, which risked being misinterpreted, instead of dealing with a professional dispute, which he had himself raised, through the appropriate channels. This error is regrettable. We are also asked to point out that Mr Hirschfeld was not alone in attacking Mr Finlay. On the contrary, as the French authorities made clear in their official statement on the matter, Mr Finlay was the victim of a "campaign of disinformation". It is not within our competence to say whether Mr Hirschfeld was a party to this campaign.

Jessie Kesson

It Was Upon a Lammas Nicht

A sparsely furnished room in a Cottar house. In a single bed against wall, BELL BROGAN, fully recovered from delivery of baby son is sitting up drinking tea out of a chipped enamel mug. The Howdie, Murchie' for short, MRS MCMURCHIE, is arranging pieces of linen over the backs of two wooden kitchen chairs which act as a makeshift airer

Introductory music – Scots song about an unmarried mother:

> Tak the buckles fae your sheen
> Bonnie lassie O
> For our dancin days are dune
> Bonnie lassie O
> Tak the flounces fae your goon
> Mak a sarkie for your loon
> For your dancin days are dune
> Bonnie lassie O

MRS M takes a bit of linen off the chair, crosses to drawer on table containing baby, adjusts linen round baby. Straightening up, she swivels round to BELL

MRS M: (*despairingly*) O Bell. Bell Brogan. What's to become o ye! Neither crib, pram or stitch o claes for your new-born bairn. You was feckless as a quine, an the years havena changed ye…

MRS M turns and goes back to the hearth and sits down in a shabby horsehair arm chair. She picks up a bit of sewing she's been working on.

(*to BELL*) To fa for a bairn at *your* age. You must be knockin forty noo …I could *understand* it …if it had happened when you was a *quine*. Accordin to what they say about your cairryins on…

BELL bangs mug down on table. Heaves herself up in bed

BELL: (*irate*) I ken fat they say. Fine *that!* (*mimics*) *They* wad *nivir* dae This… *They* wad *nivir* dae That! Abune aa …They wad nivir dae the …Other Thing… before they got the weddin band on their finger.

MRS M: (*Drily*) And you *did*, Bell…

BELL: (*slightly subdued*) …That's just about it…

MRS M: Mair's the peety…

BELL: Ye ken fat like it is, Mistress Murchie… When the notion cam ower me I just could never say NO! Ye ken yersel…

MRS M: (*startled, offended, stops sewing*) I *dinna* ken! I dinna ken masel. Thank God. The notion nivir cam ower *Me* …If it *had I* could be lyin in *your* bed there. And I've gotten nae mind for *that!*

BELL: (*submissively*) …Ah well. Maybe ye dinna ken….)

BELL pulls herself down in bed, turns on her side, presses her face against the pillow.

(*almost to herself*) ...ye get lonesome whiles. Working in Ferm Hooses... Cut off fae quines your ain age... Lang nichts sittin by yoursel in the kitchen... Ye ken that up in the bothy the horseman is sittin by his sel... You've gotten tae ken him... You mak his bed ...sweep oot his bothy ivry day... gie him his brose in the mornins. Ye get tae ken him better than ye ken onybody else – Then he'll slip in by the kitchen at nicht ...For a newse just ...It *sterts* like that... Then ae thing leads tae anither...

MRS M: (*curious*) Ye nivir thocht o gettin wedded...

BELL: I nivir got the chance...

MRS M: Well, Bell. Ye ken fat they say ...Ye dinna need ta buy the cow when ye can get the milk for naething. Ye should have minded on *That*. There's nae excuse for ye.

MRS M sets the sewing aside, rises up. She arranges cloths airing on backs of chairs, then pokes the fire in the hearth. While she is about this 'business', where it will underscore theme but not intrude on dialogue:

MALE SINGER: (*quietly, almost voice-over*)
Tak the buckles fae your sheen
Bonnie lassie O
For your dancin days are dune
Bonnie lassie O

MRS M:
Mak the flounces fae yer goon
Mak a sarkie for your loon...

MRS M takes up teapot sitting by the hearth and tests its heat with her hand

It's still hot. (*she carries teapot over to Bell's bed and refills mug*) Nae excuse for you, Bell. Tak Meg Wylie. She's workit up in the kitchen o the Ferm Hoose for near twenty years... an has never...

Bell bangs mug down on table

Mrs M: Canny. Ye'll wauken the bairn.

MRS M makes her way back to her chair by the fire

BELL: (*annoyed*) Meg Wylie... Mim-mouthed Meg... Forever braggin that she's nivir set fit in a Dance Hall. That she canna stan the very smell o whisky... That men are just efter Ae thing – and that they've nivir gotten it fae *Her!*

She lifts up mug of tea again:

(*grinning, reflective*) I doot if onybody wad want it fae Her!

MRS M: Ye canna condemn Meg for *that*. It's jist in her nature.

BELL: She's aye condemning Me. And it's jist in *my* nature...

Hurried footsteps sound from outside window. Rap on window. MRS M, setting curtain slightly, peers out

MRS M: Speak aboot the Devil! It's Hersel...

Door is flung open. MEG WYLIE rushes in, carrying a paper parcel. She leans against the door getting her breath back.

MRS M: Has that bull gotten loose again?

MEG: (*still breathless*) Nae the *bull* ...the *horsemen!* ...the pair o them. They've just got off the toon bus. ...As drunk as pipers ...I thought ...I thought they'd catch up on me...

MRS M: It's Term Nicht ...They're *entitled* to drink on Term Nicht.

BELL: Poor buggers. It's the only nicht they can afford a drink.

MEG pushes aside curtain and opens the window slightly. Indistinct singing is heard from a distance. MEG shuts window

MEG: Wad ye listen to *that!*. Ye'll be in for a nicht o't!

MRS M goes quietly to the door and opens it slightly. The horsemen's song becomes more distinct:

>When I gang tae the Kirk on Sunday
>Mony's the bonny lass I see
>Sittin by her faither's side
>An mony's the walk she's haen wi me.
>Some can drink an no get drunk
>Some can fecht an no be slain.

MRS M shuts the door, lifts the paper parcel that MEG has set down on a small table in front of the window

MRS M: Fit's this then?

MEG: Some bits and pieces o her last bairn's the Mistress thocht you micht mak use o...(*sotto voce*) Seein... *she's*... had nae foresicht...

MEG goes over to BELL's bedside

SO!! ...You've dune it *this* time Bell. Filed in your ain nest.

MRS M: (*from table where she's examining articles from the parcel. Sharply*) Bell's nae the *First*. And certain it *is* ...She'll nae be the last.

MEG turns down covers for a long peer at baby in wooden drawer. She straightens up to look at BELL

MEG: The bairn doesna favour *you*.

MEG bends to look at the bairn again. Speaks to bairn – for BELL's benefit

No... Ye dinna take after your mither ...your ...faither, maybe...? It's ...faither... Maybe ...eh? ...Is that it?

BELL: ...If ye kent *wha* his faither was... Is *that* it, Meg?

MEG straightens up sharply. Makes for table beside MRS M

MEG: (*snorting as she goes*) I'm nae concerned one wye or the ither! It's *your* worry. (*To MRS M, but also intended for BELL's ears*) ...And worry it'll be for her ...the Mistress says they're on the lookoot for somebody tae tak her place in the dairy...

BELL: (*shooting straight up in bed*) The *Mistress* says! She *does*, does she! Lat me tell *you* something. Her Man says different. And *He's* the boss...

MRS M and MEG suddenly stiffen up at table. Their eyes catching each others'. BELL interprets the "look"

NO! He's *nae* the faither o my bairn. He's keepin me on becaue I dae a man's job up in that dairy for *half* the wage a man wad cost him. As soon's I get a pram...

MEG: When ye get a pram?

MRS M: I micht manage tae dae something about *that* for you, Bell. I'll hae a word wi Jean Gartly. Poor Jean.

MEG: I heard tell she lost her bairn.

MRS M: An waur than that she canna have anither... She'll hae nae need o a pram noo. I'll hae a word wi Jean...

MEG: (sharply) Better you nor ME! Jean Gartly michtna be in a *mind* tae hand ower her pram for a bairn that was sair wanted tae a bairn that was...

BELL: (in instantly) My bairn wasna *intended,* Meg, but noo that I've gotten it, it *is* wanted. And it will nae be withoot a pram!

MRS M, momentarily in sympathy with Bell, grabs an item of clothing brought by Meg from table and holds it up for inspection

MRS M: (to MEG) This thing wadna fit a bairn's doll, Meg! Ye've shrunk it in the washin! Rinsed them oot in *Hot* watter! *(She flings article down on table)*

Indistinct singing heard outside door. Door opens. DOD, horseman, dram taken but not inebriated – woosily amiable – sings himself in. Old bothy ballad:

DOD: Some can drink an nae be drunk,
Some can fecht an nae be slain

He is followed by DAVE, second horseman, who takes up song with him

DAVE: But I can kiss anither lad's lass
An still be welcome tae my ain.

MEG makes a sudden breenge to get out of door. Horsemen try to bar her way with jocular teasing

DOD: Ye're nae *Awa,* Meg! We'll ...convoy ...ye. *(to DAVE) Right,* Dave! We'll convoy ...Meg...

MEG, with one forceful breenge past them, 'escapes', slamming door behind her. ALL inside room overcome by laughter

DOD: Meg was safe *enough,* Mistress Murchie. That richt, Dave! She was safe enough fae you an me ...we *couldna.* Nae even if we *wanted* to...An we didna *want* to ...Richt Dave?

DOD now makes his way across to BELL's bedside

(to BELL) ...Aye then, Bell ...It's a loon, they tell me...

DOD bends over drawer, peers down at baby, straightens up, fumbles in his pocket and draws out a handful of loose change. He attempts to put it under BELL's pillow

DOD: (*to BELL*) ...Here ye are ...Here ye are, quine... Hansel... A hansel for the bairn...

Money scatters on the floor. DAVE now approaches BELL's bed. He fumbles in his pockets and takes out a handful of change

DAVE: (*to BELL*) ...Here, quine... Long life... Health...

MRS M: (*irate*) ...Put it on the table!

DAVE whirls round to do so; money scatters on floor

MRS M: For goodness sakes! ...Leave it on the *fleer*. Ye'll hae the bairn *waukened!*

DOD and DAVE make their way across to the window. DOD whips out a half-emptied half-bottle of whisky and offers it to MRS M

DOD: Ye'll hae a nip, Mistress? ...tae wet the bairn's heid?

MRS M rejects the offer with a sharp gesture of her hand

DOD: I'll no tak a refusal ...It's an ...*occasion* ...Mistress, we *maun* weet the bairn's heid.

MRS M: (*very sharply*) You want tae weet *your* heid, Dod Simmers – in the horses' trough!
(*persuasively now*) Come on... Come on noo, Lads. Bell needs her sleep. (*piloting the men cannily to the door*) Come on noo... There'll be nae word o this at yokin time ...at five o'clock in the mornin... Awa wi ye noo...

DOD AND DAVE depart equably. Mrs M shuts the door behind them and leans against the wall, tired

MRS M: Weel weel... weel then...

She recovers herself, crosses to Bell's bedside, gathers the money up from the floor, puts it on Bell's table, surveys it.

(*to BELL*) ...When the drink's in the wit's oot... they've been generous... there's enough here to buy a second-hand pram. ...I'll say *that* for them, they've been generous...

BELL: (*very matter-of-fact*) Deil the *generosity* – it's jist conscience money.

MRS M: (*bemused*) *Conscience* money?

BELL: *Conscience* money. They're wondering which ane o them faithered my bairn ...And to tell ye the *truth*, between you an me, Mistress Murchie, I dinna ken masel.

Mrs M stands stock still, speechless, for a moment. Then she puts the skeck on the door, goes to her chair by the fire, turns down the lamp on the table, and eases herself down for the night.

Full-throated singers:

Tak the Buckles fae yer sheen
etc

Photograph of Jessie Kesson by Alastair Scott

Brian Whittingham

Quality counts

The line assembly workers
always griped,
that due to

lousy design
and a press shop
that could never get it right
and plans that were *not* clear

it was no wonder
the stainless steel units
ended up with
sharp edges and
gaps that
you could poke your head through
and with loopy delivery dates
that could never be met
and a crazy management
that now expected the men
to work
right up to stopping time,
it was inevitable
the quality produced
by these skilled line workers
was bound to be
well below par

unless someone required
a wrought iron garden gate,
a made-to-measure plinth
for their electric fire
or timber for a two-apartment
rabbit hutch

then extremely accurate tolerances,
a finish of the highest quality,
and immediate delivery
would be the order of the day

these line assembly workers
understood
the importance
of a homer.

Colours

The draughtsman
told the manager
the units should be white,

"white", he said,
"they should be white!"

the manager simmered
uncontrollably,
screaming,
"brown they should be brown!

the job sheet defines
they are,

watch   my   lips

B. R. O. W. N.
brown."

as the guys
on the build line
jived
to Rock Around the Clock

because
they were on
an all-nighter
at double time and
there was only half an hour
to stopping time.

The office boy

Filed card after card
after card after card

made tea and coffee
as and when he was told

delivered plans
to very *important* people

played shove-ha'penny
with expressive skill

watched men
at the pitch and toss

listened to exploits
of drinkers and shaggers

dreamed of being
a *m a r i n e   e n g i n e e r*

and sat beside
an old ratefixer
who always told him
how he would like a bowl
of the secretary's bathwater
for his soup.

Daylight

The welder would
        d r a g his
        early morning cable
        to the dockside welding pots

        argue like
        a banshee
        about which one was his

        climb below
        steel decks and squeeze
        into confined space, legs first.

for hours on end
he watched
sparks igniting
like long play fireworks

Occasionally
he snapped
open the metal lid
of his Golden Virginia,
and expertly rolled
an ever-so-slim cigarette,

and realise once again
a nightshift
cat had done a piss

        and at dinner
        time when he surfaced

        he would rest his head
        against a rusty pillow

        close his eyelids
        and feel
        the summer sun
        cleanse his face.

        as weeds twined
        stockyard pipes

        and a Red Admiral
        jived to the drone
        of a honey bee.

Talking to Billy

George Pryde

Pat slammed the door and stood for a minute on the landing regaining her temper. She glared at the varnished door with tartan nameplate sitting slightly askew above the letter box, gave it a kick then bumped the buggy down four flights of stairs. At the closemouth she glanced up at the window, but he was not there. She looked along the street where a few rusting cars with flat tyres rested against the kerb.

"Right, Billy," she said, tucking the blanket tightly around his body, "let's go and see your granny." She walked the buggy downhill towards the roundabout. In the distance to the north the Campsie Fells were sharp and clear, the Glen a bright green in the morning sun. Two doubledecker buses groaned as they climbed the hill. The trees in Kings Park were black and bare. "Jeez, it's cold!" She rubbed her hands down her anorak. "Why didn't Ah mind ma gloves, Billy?" she said. "Too much o a rush to get out that bloody house." She stamped her feet hard. "At least Ah minded the boots. You OK, wee man?"

He gazed up at her wide eyed, his nose a red button in a white face. "Pull that collar up a bit," she said, stopping, restraining the buggy handle with her elbows as she adjusted his anorak. "We've a long way to go, and it's gonny get colder. Be a lot handier if your granny stayed roon the corner." She gripped the handle, allowing the buggy to roll down the hill. At the roundabout she waited as a line of cars streamed by, turning off up the hill to Castlemilk or downhill to Kingspark, Govanhill, Glasgow Cross.

"They've aa got cars, Billy. We can hardly afford your buggy. Nae justice, son. Nae justice." She crossed the road and pushed up the slight gradient, then down by Kings Park. "I suppose we could go in – would you like that, Billy?" He looked up at her, face expressionless. "Naw, don't suppose you would today – maybe in a couple of months. March is a cauld yin." She smiled. "Your Da and I had good times in there, Billy. Seems like a lifetime ago." God, she thought, gazing through the railing, how did we let it get to this state? Eighteen months each one worse than the last.

She pointed: "That was where you were started, up in among the big trees. Now we've got tae live wi the consequences, you and me, and your Da too, I suppose. He's a right bastard your Da. Good job you don't understand yet, but you will, son, you will." She continued, past the funeral home and along towards Hampden Park. On the left she gazed at the large red sandstone villas with their wide-fronted lawns. "There's money for you, Billy. One day, you never know. If he'd only get a job. Ah know it's not easy, no wi this lot in. Still, he could try harder. Hughie across the landing managed tae get something – no much but better than nothin, better than dole money, Income Support. Anything's better than that, son." I'm kidding myself, she thought. Us livin in a place like that – even if he got a job.

At Mount Florida she stopped and looked into shop windows. "Look at that three piece suite, Billy, look at it! Aa we need's money, that's aa. Know any banks we could rob, eh? You and me, Billy the Kid and his Mammy!"

She crossed Prospecthill Road. "Downhill all the way, Billy. Wonder why they called it Mount Florida? A bit exotic, don't you think – Ah mean for Glasgow." He smiled. "Glad you agree. Or was that wind you had there? You're worse than your Da. When we get to your granny's we'll have something nice to eat, she always has soup ready. Why Mount *Florida*? What your Ma disnae know could fill a library, son. Dead ignorant, I am. Hope you dinnae take after me or your Da. That lazy swine. The only sums he can dae is calculate what he gets back fae the bookie when he wins, and that's no bloody often. Gies more tae the bookie than he does tae you and me. Knows the bookie better tae, if you ask me."

At Crosshill she walked between the grey sandstone tenements. "When Ah was younger, Billy, Ah didnae like this bit. It was like walking through a canyon, dark and grimy. Now it's been cleaned up. You can see the stone as it was when they built it. They've money for some things." She bent down and kissed her son. "Don't mind me, Billy, you know I'm no always like this. Ah'll try and cheer up, for you. Might even manage tae cheer maself at the same time. Never mind, we're almost there."

At the gushet she crossed the road. "See, there's your granny's flat, ten storeys up – no much longer. Down there used to be Gorbals Cross, with a clock on the island in the centre – so your granny says. I dinnae mind it."

When she reached the flats she pushed in through the entrance door and stood waiting at the lift. An old woman was standing with a small shopping bag grasped tightly in her hand. "Just down for a few wee things, hen," she said. "Got tae get out once a day at least. Visiting?...Your Mammy?"

"Ay, tenth floor."

"Thought you were – but some o the young yins here move so much sometimes it's hard to know if they stay here or no."

Pat looked at the lights as the lift descended from the twelfth floor. It stopped, the door scraped open. "In you go, hen, get your wean in first." The woman held the door. "Don't want some bugger trying to get it before we get in." The door closed: "Ten was it?" She pressed the button. "I'm on the fourteenth. Rare view from there." The lift lurched its way up. "Look at that, dirty swines!" The woman pointed to the corner. "Thought I smelt something. Wasn't there when I came down. Bloody kids!"

At the tenth, Pat pushed the buggy out onto the landing. "Cheerio, Mrs!" As the door closed she bent to her son. "Well, we're here, Billy. A wee cup of tea and a bun, eh!" She pressed the buzzer. The sound rasped through the flat. As she waited she tidied the anorak and blanket around her son. "God, she's gettin' deaf, your granny!" She pressed again, and stood back waiting. The flat was silent. No familiar sound of the inside door opening, her mother coughing. Silence, except for Billy wheezing. "Shite!"

She went back to the lift. "All this way for her tae be oot. Well we're no goin back, no yet. Prob'ly down at the shops, but we're no standin here like doolies waitin. We'll go into town – how about the St Enoch Centre, at least that'll be warm."

Crossing the suspension bridge Pat stopped in the middle and looked downriver. The Clyde was grey, with a freezing wind coming from the distant Firth. "Better get a move on, Billy." She jumped up and down. "Feel the bridge moving, wee man?"

In St Enoch Square she stood looking up the steps at the entrance to the Centre. "They didnae think about mothers wi kids when they designed this, did they, son? I've got to lug you and this buggy up aa they steps." A woman stopped. "I'd give you a hand, but my back –" She rubbed her back to emphasise the point. "If you go along to the other end there's a ramp. He's a nice looking boy, aren't you son? I wish I was your age again." She smiled and went up the steps.

"Ay, right, Mrs," murmured Pat, "at least your man would've had a job." She trundled the buggy over the pink cobblestones up the ramp and into the Centre. It was warm, airy, and she pushed the buggy across the shiny marble floor, looking in department store windows. On the first floor she paused at a travel agent. "Where will it be this year, Billy – Florida or Saltcoats. God how I hated Saltcoats, your granny loved it." She pushed on into a store. It was busy, with people stopping suddenly in her path. "Christ," she said, "this is murder. Let's get out of here, Billy. I hope your granny is in."

At the flat door she pressed the buzzer and listened intently. Silence. "Surely tae God!" She pressed again. There was the sound of a cistern flushing, then her mother's shuffle in the hall. The door opened. "Oh, it's you – the bell always goes when I'm in there. Come in, I'm not long in myself."

"I know," said Pat, lifting Billy from the buggy and sitting him on the carpet in front of the electric fire. "We came up an hour ago."

"You should have phoned, Pat. I was just down at Mrs Mackay's on the second floor."

"The phone's not working."

"It's like that is it?"

"Priorities, Ma. Wi no a lot tae play wi you've got tae have priorities and the phone's at the bottom of the list."

"All you have to do is ask, Patricia. That's what I'm here for. You know I've a bit spare – ask."

Pat pulled off Billy's anorak and sat him back down with a teddy. "We have enough, Ma. We get by."

"What would you do in an emergency – suppose you need a doctor in a hurry for Billy – what'll you do?"

"Go next door – they've a phone. It's no *that* important, Ma – other things come first. We do get by, it's just that now and then it gets a bit tight."

"Ay, well... here, he's too near the fire, look he's like a beetroot – move him away."

Pat lifted Billy clear of the fire. "He's all right."

"Still not talking, is he?"

"Boys are slower. He'll make up for it when he's older. They aa dae. As long as he's no like his Da – every fourth word he says begins wi an eff."

"Ay, I warned you. If you make your bed you have to –"

"Ah know, Ah know. And Ah do. No as much as he does though. Aa he gets out o it for is either the bookie or the pub. Anyway, we've enough to last till the next cheque, that's aa that matters."

"Ay, well alright, but let me know if you're short. Here, I've a bun in the bread tin from yesterday. It should still be soft, so I'll half it and give it to Billy. I'll heat up some soup for you both. Could do with a bit myself." She went into the kitchen. "And are you getting on OK, the two of you?"

Pat sighed. "We get by, Ma."

"But he's still going into the bookies and the pubs?"

"Ah've just said so. It leaves us a bit short, but we get there. He's no a responsible bloke but he's no a bad man."

Ay, she thought, he used to be great fun to be with, always laughing, was considerable in a rough sort of way, but now...

Her mother clattered soup plates in the kitchen. "It'll be ready in a minute. Your father was like that. He wasn't a bad man either. Liked his pint – just like the rest of them. They all have to prove themselves. You're no a man unless you can walk home wi half a dozen whiskies inside you and God knows how many pints. You're no alone, Patricia. I've been through it too, I know what it's like to be skint before payday." She came into the room with two plates of soup. "Get stuck into this, I'll bring bread and a wee plateful for Billy."

When she sat down at the fire with the plate in her lap, she ruffled Billy's head. "He's a nice boy, I'm sure he'll turn out better than his father."

"Widnae be hard, Ma."

"Is he giving you enough money?"

Pat dipped bread into her soup. "Ay, if he's had to come straight back, usually 'cause he's left his line. Spends hours choosing his horses."

"Well in future go with him to the post office, get the money from him even if you have to create a scene. Stand there and shout at him. He'll soon cough up. They don't like scenes in public. But they need a bit of dignity so make sure he has something in his pocket. It's a fine balance, Patricia, it's up to you." She put the empty plate on the table. "That soup was nice, even though I say it myself. Up you come, Billy." She took him on her knee and fed him soup with a teaspoon. "That's the boy!"

I know what he needs, thought Pat, and it's no bloody dignity. She looked at the clock on the mantlepiece. "Better get back before it gets dark, Ma." She stood, brushing crumbs from her lap. "Thanks for the soup."

"Ay, he's getting tired, wee soul."

"No a wee soul if he sleeps too early and gets me up at six! Anyway, I'd better go." She slipped his anorak on him, struggling with his flailing arms. "Now, into your buggy, and and stop whingein!" She strapped him in.

"I'll see you to the bus."

"No, Ma, it's too cold, there's no need."

"Nonsense. Wait till I get my coat."

"We're walking back, Ma. So there's no need."

"Walking! It's uphill all the way. Are you *that* short?"

Pat shrugged. Christ, she thought, we're no goin through this again? "We walked down, Ma. It was nice and fresh. Billy enjoyed the air. We'll walk back. It's no the money – honest. We like walking, keeps us healthy, doesn't it, Billy. As long as he's wrapped up, Ma, he'll be fine. You worry too much."

"I'd worry less if you took the bus."

"See me to the lift so that I can get in. That's far enough. OK?"

"Ay, well, if you insist. But I'd rather you –"

"No, Ma, we're fine, honest. It'll keep us out of the house a bit longer, anyway."

"Jesus, what an excuse!"

"We get by, Ma. We get there."

She pushed the buggy through the entrance door to the flats. "God it's freezin'!" She stopped and pulled Billy's anorak higher around his neck. "Could get snow yet, Billy." She looked up the vertical wall of the flats. A hand waved through the opening in a window on the tenth floor.

At the gushet she crossed the road and began the uphill climb. When she reached Crosshill she stopped. "Better take a breather, Billy, we've a long way to go, yet." She bent towards him. "You OK, wee man? Ay, you look warm enough." She took out her purse, opened it and rifled through each part. "Just hoping for a miracle, Billy, but nothing doing. Enough to keep us till Thursday – if I'm careful. No enough for bus fares, son." She straightened up and began to push again. "Not be long, Billy. Mount Florida, up by the park, then up the big hill. Thirty five minutes if I walk fast – no be long. Hope tae Christ your Da's out. I could dae wi a bit o peace. She kissed his cold face. "If Ah didnae talk to you, Billy, who would Ah talk tae?"

Tom Hubbard

Berlioz at Meylan

1. Stella Montis

Look closely at the small silent one
With the big noise inside him.
Speak to him; – he averts his dark eyes,
Mutters fretfully, impatiently.
There is a party at his grandfather's house,
There is laughter in every room and in the garden.
The swish of the skirts, too much, too much:
His collar tightens, he must outside.

Under his favourite tree, he reads Cervantes.
He finds comfort in the faithful fuddled Don.
They would shake their heads, his elders, smilingly,
– With a gentle warning perhaps,
If they knew the turn of his thoughts.
He is a knight of the rocky glen:
He halts his steed by the spring
Hears voices from the ruined tower –
"Poor Hector! His head is full of Walter Scott!"

So the dream breaks, brutally, as always.
Is that his uncle, and the sound of his spurs,
Is that his uncle, dancing with *her*?
Oh, the anguish of a boy of twelve
Gazing at a woman of eighteen!
And then the game, and the taking sides:
Each cavalier must choose his partner.
The boy blushes, he cannot hide.
"*I'll* choose," she says, and sparkles near to him.
"This is my beau – let me present to you
My own Monsieur Hector."

Quivering in the nest,
The future eagle of the alps
Is a tiny, wounded lark.

2. Nocturne

It is cool on the heights of Meylan.
Two women recline on marble;
One questions, the other replies,
Their voices join in the evening quiver.

– Vous soupirez, madame?

Beyond, across the valley,
The moon brings forth the mountain snows; the chain
Of Belledonne looms through the mise-en-scène
Of the challenged ones: who brood with troops of friends
Marching between rocks and lakes, hoping, expecting
The gates of Grenoble, opened; and those, more prey than eagle,
Who dodge in cave and cellar
Getting the message (and the men) through, the women
as brave and braver,
Watchful throughout the passion of the times
For that merely changing gesture of a comrade
That leads at last to death at the roadside wall:
Casting their blood, where, later, children lay flowers
– Yet a loved lady bemoans her heavy hours!

– Quoi! Vous pleurez, madame?

Yes, weeping for empires, pacts, betrayals.

The moon brings forth, over the terrace,
The statue of a mother and son:
Two women recline on marble;
One questions, the other replies.

3. Le Rouge et le Noir

With the energy of Faust
With the laughter of Mephistopheles
The man of the rocks
Is scornful of Paris,
Frigid, effete
– Though Harriet played there!

Poor Harriet, perfervid Celt,
As Juliet, Ophelia,
Revealed all Shakespeare
To the amorous Dauphinois.

(– *"Romanticism pleases French Shakespeareans,
But Classicism pleases their great-grandads."*
And Metropolitanism's
For metropoltroons.)

Ah!... if only the harshness
Between Hector and Harriet
Had never been more
Than the crazy raillery
Between Béatrice and Bénédict:

And yet ... no pistol-shot,
As when Julien Sorel
Felled Madame de Rênal:
Hector ascends not the scaffold
But more familiar slopes;
His head has long been greying
With earlier hopes.

Hector, dark wanderer,
Again to Meylan bound,
With all his love's labours
Not lost, but unfound.

4. Ripeness is All

Having pursued his Damnation
Across Europe,
In Breslau, Passau,
Vienna, Pest;
Leaving his bed, in Prague,
Writing in the middle of the night
The apotheosis of Marguerite:

"Remonte au ciel, âme naïve
Que l'amour égara."

Having called up demons
From the orchestra pit,
Tones that before
Were uncombined, unheard;
Magic at court for every Emperor
Except the chancer of the Tuileries,
Whose alchemists are borrowed from the Bourse;

Having soothed, stirred or scorned
The ears of Europe:
For him, *the insubstantial pageant faded*
Leaves not a wrack behind ...he seeks the stone,
The stone where once Estelle, taking his hand,
Had crossed the mountain stream. Here, his true voice

Unites itself, as ever,
to forests, crags and torrents: heights of Meylan,
So much in place a quarter-century on,
Save that Estelle has gone –

– To Lyon.

See him now, at sixty-one,
Only a few years remaining to him;
Not as far-gone as Lear, but certainly
A fond foolish old child, who "is not reasonable";
(Neither sane, nor insane, but a-sane...)
"We shall meet," she writes, "after my son's wedding;
I am very touched by your feelings ... all these years."

He is the happiest of hosts to Estelle's boy
And his bride:
This Prospero finds a Ferdinand and Miranda.

The return to life: but the last episodes
In the life of the artist. Hector seeks Estelle
Now in Geneva. Walks by the lakeside gardens,
The steamers both absorbing and emitting
Assorted English burghers, with toy-wives;
Here a Falstaff, much more sober, still as fat;
There a Caliban, with his top hat and cane.

Hector proposes, and Estelle declines.
They look to Mont Salève; perhaps their thoughts
Are further south... to Meylan: there, too early,
And here, too late, too late...

The Seat at the Front

Linda McCann

She's not in. I'll just have a wee seat over here for a minute, have a look at the sea – oh look at all that dust – I mean the way the sand's all blown along into the slats – see that, all collected there.

Well I could be doing with a rest. Doreen'll not be long – I mean she says Mum she says give me a phone and let me know when you're coming but och if you can't just drop in on your own daughter it's a bad day.

That's her window up there, see it? The one with the pink curtains – they were no good to me, too small for my windows when I moved here. I'm just along the road there, nice an handy.

It's a wonder I didn't pass her the now – I came along the main road just in case she was away out – she'll not've went far, maybe along at the shops – see Doreen'll not let anyone help her any more – the both of us used to get the shopping done in no time but now she's that – independent.

And I mean that's another thing. See they curtains I gave her? Well they're no up right. Plumber put them up for her. Oh there's no telling her but – up with a spirit level she says: away to the wan side like Gourock more like. My heart's roasted with her. Her taste used to be all Habitat, that clean, an now I mean for a start here's this picture up in her hall, soon as you walk in, right dark and stoorey-lookin – it was lying in her cupboard when she moved in she says, just this old picture an a perr a dirty knickers – well I says you'd a been as well pittin up the knickers.

Ay, I don't know what's keeping her the day. It's a lovely day isn't it? I mean it's not too hot – it's nice and fresh.

It's a lovely house she's got – lovely flat. That's all she needs, all decorated as well – she'd only to do the bathroom. Whole flat's papered in thon fancy stuff – what d'you call that? – you know, old-fashioned – it's a woman's name, eh, wee teeny flooers. It was lucky – I saw the advert in the estate agent's window, phoned her, and she was right through on the train, got her survey done the next morning. Yes. She's done awful well – no worries about nothin – paid cash for it.

She could've got a lot more you know, out of the divorce settlement – oh ay, could've forced him to sell his business, give her half. She didn't want that though.

She's got a beautiful view, hasn't she? Beautiful outlook. That's all she sees, all that sea for miles and miles, right across to Ireland: so peaceful.

Oh thone was terrible the other day – oh. They ambulancemen had an awful job getting the door open with Doreen lying behind it. Ay. She must've just heard that nosey neighbour a hers ringing the bell and then tripped and hit her head when she went to answer it, knocked herself out.

And I mean see that neighbour a hers? – dead pally and Doreen thinks she's awfy-nice but I could see right through her. Well she comes up, right – Doreen had been telling her about her new bathroom, and I mean it's lovely, floor to ceiling in three different kinds of tile or is it four – but the neighbour says oh she says it's like the Taj Mahal. So I says well after all it's what you like yourself isn't it? – cheek a her eh? Oach, fur coat an nae knickers I mean that's the kind that'll tell you it's got a jacuzzi if it broke a bit wind in the bath.

No, it's just been a wee bad patch Doreen's been going through, with the divorce an that. That was her divorce became final the other day.

And she'd been awful sick you know when the ambulancemen got her, awful sick all over the place, a right touch of the boil, you know, and well – she'd had a wee diarrhoea. It was all they pills she'd had – not so good to take a drink when you're taking medicine. Ay, it's been a pity for her, this wee illness.

And it is an illness you know – noo-look – she went to AA – lot a queeries – all lawyers, ministers and nuns – a dis-grace – all sittin ther that smug an shakin yir hand an washin thir manky habits in public – that would make you take a drink so it would – Doreen I said, you'd be as well up the road and have a nice cup a coffee, stead a that tea they geed us – hot water knocked stupit, sittin ther listenin to that.

She makes a lovely cup of coffee on that machine I got her, wee house-warming present. That's all she takes now, just coffees. Doesn't even take anything in it, milk nor sugar, just black. I mean she'll be okay here – all that carry-on with the drink, that was all her fancy so-called friends.

Lovely the sound of the sea, isn't it?

Yes, she's probly away along to the delicatessen for her coffee the now. Nothing but the best.

'She' wasn't long moving in with him though – right in she was, soon as Doreen left (course they wereny in that house long because he had to sell it) but that's them – married – few hours ago this afternoon – that was the big day the day – didny waste any time once the divorce came through.

He was seeing 'hur' for years you know – I had a wee house at the end of their road but we never knew a thing about it.

This is me just back from Glasgow the now matter of fact – I came right along here. Doreen'll be wanting all the details.

Oh yes, I was at the wedding – I mean I couldn't resist going for a look – anyone can go to a wedding, you know – so I just sat at the back, good view of all the people.

Course the lassie's father wisny there – ay you never know the minute, eh? – awfa nice man – seemingly hur mother was knocking about a bit, well you don't know what to believe – but big shock – there I was the one minute, talking to him at the bus stop quite the thing – ach, he seemed a bit fed up. I mean aren't we all? and I says cheerio keep taking the tablets, next thing, I hears he tane an overdose – jist shows you. I sent a wee card.

Well listen – you should have saw the money at that wedding – Mr Big Businessman – they certainly never stood on ceremony – hired a castle, if you don't mind – turrets, flags and that – two coachloads of us out by Loch Lomond for a blessing then back to the Ivan ho-ho -tel. Course I never went to the meal – wouldny have been right.

And of course allow her – she'd the cheek to wear white. Lovely bride right enough if you like that kind a thing – she was aye that thin – no bust, you know. Nothing. And with that tight wedding dress really she was like a poor wee bandaged fing-er. Oh don't get me wrong – quite pretty in a smiling doll sort of way – with they ear-to-ear teeth – she aye had that mooth you could post parcels in – and that wee turned-up nose she's got, all red at the end by getting squeezed with all the smiling.

And no make-up on either. Well – I really think that to wear no make-up at all on your own wedding day is just sheer arrogance. I mean with that wee pale face and that cadaverous grin – and the head-dress? – her hair was all tucked away under a white band right down over her forehead like a nun – no, between you and me she'd really have been better away stalkin the battlements.

But see the money? – the guests? – such expensive people – and the wedding dress? – oh, richly embroidered – all covered in they tearoom designs – you know thon, eh, in Sauchiehall Street with the square roses and the ladderback chairs? – Willow Pattern Tearoom – used to go in there myself all the time, matter of fact – oh and she'd a see-through polo-neck an all an that wee sticky-oot chin of hers hooked right over the top of it, and the bodice was that tight, right into the ribs it was – ay, like a ladder-front – (oh here I mind the name a that paper – Anna Glypta – ay I knew it was a wummin's name). But don't get me wrong – good luck to the lassie right enough – she'll need it wi him – I wouldny give you tuppence for him for all his money – Doreen's father was the same first chance he got, and every chance after that.

But oh Doreen was the perfect mother. That granddaughter of mine had the best of everything, beautiful wee froacks imported from Paris, and the image of Doreen so she was.

All 'he' ever thought about was teeth, all his clients – best clients in Scotland you know, very upper-crust – I bet he wiped the smiles off their faces, bored the money out a them probably. Ay, well he's got plenty a bloody teeth to look at noo.

No, Doreen's much better off away from him.

And that's my granddaughter talking about getting engaged to that boyfriend of hers now. And I mean that boy's just stacking shelves in a shop (although it is Marks and Spencer's right enough). No, but she can do a lot better than that, just doesn't know her own mind yet.

I wonder what's keepin ma Doreen but. Funny – she never was this late before. I wondered if she was maybe away for a wee sleep. No but she wouldny sleep during the day – I mean she's not that kind of person.

Here it's a bit nippy gettin. Don't tell me that's the rain on. She can't be long now. Oh well, it's not every day your ex-husband marries your ex-best friend, is it? Doreen'll be dying to hear all about the wedding.

Oh my God – the noise of they new ambulances? Goes right through you so it does.

Ay, she's landed on her feet right enough, can start afresh. She's got nothing to pay.

Peter Snow

Fear

Old snakes outlive their poison
They dart their impotent flat heads
At shadows; still we walk wide
Of their cold, hidden beds:
Malice coiled in their hide
And eyes a plentiful bad foison.

Special Offer

He waits in the desert for the healer,
Wings wrapped tight as a tout's mac,

Heels driving, toeclaws gouging, deep.
Stones into bread, miracle, power;

To and fro, on the hot, disregarded earth,
The serpent floods his poison sacs;

Aware that venom turns to medicine
In the healer's hands.

Hopeful of success, or failure,
He waits in the desert for the healer.

Asthma

Last night the water rose
past our windows. The sun
twists and bulges above the surface.

Fish are everywhere; they nose round corners,
pouring in startling shoals out of closes,
nudging under cars and spiralling

up the staircases of buses.
They dart away from dirty boiling
out of drains, and hide among the branches

of the city trees. There is a distant
and mysterious orchestra,
but the rhythm of the undertow is stronger

and compelling downwards. My ribs
will spring apart like bucket handles,
my organs will unfurl and waft like ugly plants.

Frightened awake I am clenched
tight in a burst accordion,
and all the bright fish are gone.

Men have walked over the moon

The Goblin Prince, when the moonlight shone,
With drums and flutes he urged us on;
There was magic under the moon.

But the night of the Goblin Prince is gone,
He has vanished away into stick and stone;
The magic since is man's alone.
It has conjured him up to the moon

Which hangs in the morning pale and wan,
For men have walked over the moon.

But the Goblin waits in stick and stone.
"Lo, how my magic all has grown!
Soon I shall claim it back as my own.
I shall rise and be terrible, very soon."

Isobel Grant Stewart

Snow in the Suburbs by Thomas Hardy

Ilka branch grat wi it
A the birks booed wi it
Ilka wee crummockie lik a duik fit
Nivir a soun in loanin an wynd
The drifflin flakes hae gaen agley an tyne thair gait
An mell thairsels wi ither draps
Ti gen the grund
The palins glaur'd thegither lik a dyke
Wi nae baff o wun i the saftlin fa.

A speug cams ben the tree
An aa at aince
A clod o snaw, by-ornar grat,
Fas ower his heid an glabbers ower his een
An dings him heid bi dowp
An gey neir smoors him
An fas on a laigher branch, whaur its blash
Caas off a the ither clods wi a breengin clash.

The stairs are aa wan stey brae
Whaur, scrawny, dowf an wae
A black cat sclims wi gawpin een
An we tak him ben.

Sandy Harvey

Arran

I have often contrived
to cauterize my thoughts
into a hard poetry,
a fine-toothed ridge
like theses unstinting spines
that broke the sea's back.

I have often vowed
to set my face,
a sullen stone
hard against the winds
that tunnel these crags
and hone their peaks.

I would forget love
with its wild, tortured hopes,
the sea bird's elemental cry
the only song to issue
forth from the rock
the steels my heart's core.

Yet in the final irony
it is these great spurs
in their sun-crowned glory
that melt the heart's fetters
and blast the ice-rime
from the rim of the soul's crater.

Young working class mother

I mind o you frae the skuill,
Ye widnae gang oot wi me –
said I wisnae your type,
I wisnae "intae" the discos.
Nae doobt ye were richt
but I see ye got yuir man –
the bairn made siccar o that,
an hou he lo'es that bairn!
Sees the future's bricht sterne
in his ocean blue een,
whiles you staun in the backgrund
like an auld grey photie
hauf tint in the haars o time.
Untentit yuir hauns aa chappit

wi slaisterin tae yuir elbucks
in a sink o frozen watter
on cranreuch mornins,
untentit the fag that jouks at yuir chaft
author at aince o yuir scunner, yuir anger
an yuir wanhope untentit the thocht
channerin like a snake in yuir skull:
"That bluidie bairn wis the daith o me."

Sunday tea

Pechin ablow the deid wecht o my relatives,
cockin hauf dozent lugs at their clash
o "young yins nooadays", terrorist bombs
an the soond o pandrops bein souked in kirk,
I butter a scone
an think on a woman whase een
I could easy loup intae an droun mysel,
lettin her smoor my senses on her ocean's flair.
I bite the scone, its stourie substance
crottles doun tae mak a desert o my thrapple,
stechin the movements o my Adam's aipple,
butchin my desire in an eternal jyle.

Future

Orwell's future: the tackety buit
champin my face like a neep,
my harns floatin
on the glaur that slaisters
frae historie's blackest mools;
Yet it's no this weird's certaintie
I'm feared o maist,
but optimism's preen-heid spunk
fechtin for the gree o my hert.

Foreign tongue

(Thinking of Lewis Grassic Gibbon)

It is with alien effort I write of you
in an affected foreign tongue.
Yet, unlike you, I have refused terms with it,
Save for now
as my pen chaves like a plough
through a stony park.

CREATIVE
S P A C E

Summer School 1995
Writing – Painting – Drawing

Creative writing courses in Argyll Coast Country House.

Suitable for beginners and more experienced writers.

Full board, excellent food, small groups (max 10).

Peace and quiet in a relaxing, informal atmosphere.

For a brochure write or phone:
Lunga Mill
Ardfern
Argyll PA31 8QR
(01852) 500 526

July 1 – 8
Dylis Rose
The Whole Story
An in-depth look at short story writing

July 8 – 15
Liz Lochhead
Image into Voice
For poets and short prose writers

September 9 – 16
Brian McCabe
Starting to Write
Workshops on poetry, fiction and non-fiction

Not(e) from the Margin

Christopher Whyte

In January 1934 Christopher Isherwood found himself waiting outside an office in the port of Harwich in East Anglia, England. His lover Heinz was due to arrive. Hitler was in power in Heinz's native Germany, so he shared the danger threatening any man engaging in homosexual relations under a Nazi regime. Hitler's belligerent attitude made the onset of war more of a probability. Christopher, quivering with impatience, was summoned into the office. Heinz's luggage and person had been meticulously searched and a letter discovered which hinted at the nature of their relationship. His lover was refused admission and sent back to Germany.

Auden, who accompanied Isherwood on this occasion, insisted that the officer involved was himself a closet case and that this explained the virulence of his reaction. That may have been true. I'm more concerned with what the officer was wearing. Nowadays showing your passport at customs is an extremely relaxed affair. The officer in charge may be wearing civilian clothes. But I suspect that when Christopher's lover was turned back, the officer bore the insignia of the British state, the state of which he was a subject and which not only refused to give his relationship any validation but actually branded it as criminal.

If Heinz had been a woman things would have gone very differently. Auden, also homosexual, used the ruse of marriage to rescue Thomas Mann's lesbian daughter Erika. Auden and Isherwood left England for good in January 1939 and Britten sailed for the USA in May of the same year (though he returned in April 1942). What part did the scene at Harwich docks play in Isherwood's decision to leave? If as adult males all three were included in the British state and expected to fight for it, as homosexuals they were excluded and had no right to support or protection. They were both part and not part of the nation to which they belonged.[1]

Perhaps Virginia Woolf would have accepted Isherwood, Auden and Britten as associate members of the Outsiders' Society which she describes in her polemical essay *Three Guineas* (1938). There she reflects that her country (and it is evident that England, not Britain is intended) has treated women as slaves during most of its history, denied them education and any share in material wealth, yet now insists on regular payment of sums for a protection in which she has little or no faith. (Woolf was married to a Jew and lived near to England's Channel coast. The issue of what protection the state might offer herself and her husband in the event of invasion was therefore a crucial one and may have played a part in her decision to commit suicide.) The passage concludes with a celebrated statement by one of her outsiders that "as a woman, I have no country. As a woman I want no country. As a woman my country is the world."[2]

Both women and male homosexuals had an ambivalent relation to nationality, an ambivalence rooted in gender. Isherwood and Britten had partners of the 'wrong' gender. Being a woman or homosexual (and many would be both) meant that they were not fully English, not the full shilling.

And so the trope, the literary commonplace of the sexually aberrant as inherently treacherous has a connection, albeit a twisted one, with reality. (Think of the camp German officer and his lesbian sidekick in Rossellini's *Roma città aperta* or the public schoolboy played by Rupert Everett in the recent film *Another Country*.) Women, too, have their record of treachery. I have in mind an incident from the memoirs of a Jewish woman who survived the war in Poland. (I can no longer trace the text). After the Red Army passed westwards she called in to thank a peasant woman who had offered her refuge. The peasant woman took her to the barn and showed her three German soldiers asleep. "They are the ones who need my help now," she commented. The writer was shocked. Yet the peasant woman was acting in terms of a carefully thought-out ethical position. It was not one of unconditional loyalty to one's nation in the context of a war effort.

In this essay I will be concentrating on questions of gender and sexuality. But in case readers who are neither women nor homosexual are tempted to turn the page, it is worth reflecting on the behaviour of some Scottish, male, (predominantly) heterosexual writers and intellectuals at the outbreak of the Second World War. Douglas Young suffered a prison sentence for his refusal to fight for Britain. George Campbell Hay took to the hills of Kintyre for six weeks to avoid conscription before being rounded up by the local police and packed ignominiously off to the army. Norman MacCaig was a conscientious objector. Edwin Morgan reversed his initial decision sufficiently to serve in the Medical Corps but still refused to become a combatant. Whatever the causes which prompted their decisions, (and one wonders how far Morgan's pacifism was, like Isherwood's, rooted in the nature of his desire), there is little doubt that, for these men, nationality played a role not dissimilar to that of gender in the case of the English writers. The Scots, too, were outsiders where the British (English) state and its wars were concerned.

Things are changing in Scotland and in Scottish culture. But until some fifteen years ago observers could have been forgiven for thinking that the new Scottish literature was entirely an affair of men. (The invisibility of gay and lesbian writers is so axiomatic as hardly to require comment). This was partly because of how the history of the Scottish Renaissance Movement was presented, with women as helpmates offering succour and support from the wings. I'm thinking of a photograph of Valda and young Michael striding across the Whalsay heather, presumably collecting seagull's eggs and making sure Christopher would not be disturbed at his composing. (The behaviour of MacDiarmid's two wives fits neatly with one black and white paradigm of feminine stereotypes). Or of Helen Cruickshank, stylishly if severely dressed, sitting on a park bench in Princes Street gardens, trying to figure out where to send Scotland's greatest poet next. Willa Muir was known to me for years primarily as the best thing that ever happened to Edwin and not as an author in her own write or as the one who may have done the lion's share of the translating they both lived off.

It goes deeper than biographies, however. What are we to make of a literary movement that accepts without demur a representation like this in one of its canonical texts?

> Roddie was like a pillar that she herself could lean against. More than once she had had an almost overpowering desire to let Roddie take her and so find peace for herself inside the circle of his strength. She could have wished him to break through the barrier between them... She was weak. She was terribly weak. She feared. She did not know what she wanted... She knew she could no more have stopped him than have stopped fate. Would she have desired it? Yes, often, madly... yes... she didn't know.[3]

OK, this is badly written. And it effectively proclaims a field day for men with designs on Highland widows. (Permission need not be asked. Just take it you are fate). But it goes deeper than that. Here is another Renaissance giant (and uncanonised saint) in similarly lyrical mood.

> A man's thocht like a hameless bird
> Steers atween stern and stern:
> But the thocht o' a woman bides far ben
> As she boos abune her bairn.
>
> She wudna gie the wecht o' her breist
> For a' that men micht hae;
> And the soundin' o' their thocht gangs by
> Like the whish o' windlestrae.[4]

Women are preoccupied with the basic issues of physical and emotional survival. The superstructures, such as religion and philosophy and the concept of nation, are the province of men. As you might expect, the Great Leader expressed the position more blatantly than almost anyone else:

> And nae Scot wi' a wumman lies,
> But I am he and ken, as 'twere
> A stage I've passed as he maun pass't'
> Gin he grows up, his way wi' her![5]

The drunk man briefly (but no doubt lusciously) appropriates the favours of all the women men in his category have ever slept with, while noting that dallying with women is a pastime males grow out of. He neatly defines 'being Scottish' and 'being a woman' as mutually exclusive. Further, since 'being Scottish' means 'having sex with women', homosexual men are excluded too. (Little attention has been paid to the important role at least one Scottish male couple played in the diffusion of MacDiarmid's work and the preservation of his manuscripts). There is plenty of evidence for the constant intersection of gender and national definitions:

> Scotland, when it is given to me
> As it will be
> To sing the immortal song
> The crown of all my long
> Travail with thee
> I know that in that high hour
> I'll have, and use, the power
> Sublime contempt to blend
> With its ecstatic end,
> As who, in love's embrace,

Forgetfully may frame
Above the poor slut's face
Another woman's name.[6]

Here the Great Man is 'screwing' Scotland, giving her his damnedest while in fact thinking about somebody else, in a peculiar interweaving of Puritanism and sexism. All that redeems it is the implication that MacDiarmid's nationalism was not so unthinking and instinctive as he often pretended. It turns out he generally had something else on his mind.

So, although Scottish women are not actually Scottish, at some level Scotland *is* a woman. Chris Guthrie functions as Chris Caledonia again and again in Gibbon's trilogy. The identification woman ▪ land is presented with a dazzling and seductive lyricism. But it has unsavoury implications. Land is owned and ploughed and reaped. It is bought and sold. It can't own itself. Nor can it get up and go if it doesn't like the way things are being run. It can't talk back or change its name or say that, no thank you very much, it doesn't feel like being impregnated with the seed on this particular night of the week. The (feminine) land is a non-person. It is beyond the human. I'm thinking here of the way Chris Guthrie blends into the timeless, unchanging landscape at the end or of *Grey Granite,* of Dark Mairi, Gunn's embodiment of Gaelic Scotland:

> This 'blindness' in her expression often had the air of unintelligence, and when she smiled it could be seen as a sort of weakness running thinly all over her face. To move her out of her unthinking self seemed to expose her, to show that apart from what she was unthinkingly she was very little. One might as well have exposed a stone by causing it to smile or a piece of a mountain. Indeed, in her steady unthinking darkness, she might have walked out of a mountain and might walk into it again, leaving no sign.[7]

Whatever Mairi may be, she is not an intellectual. Gaelic culture (like women's culture) is destined to remain off the records, to disappear from the world leaving no trace of its passing.

I've quoted male authors so far. These authors saw nothing problematic in their representations of gender. Reading their work in the 1990s, we may differ from them, while still finding their representations a fascinating object of study. Women of that generation saw the problems and identified them more directly. Catherine Carswell's first, rather unsatisfactory novel *Open the Door* indulges in a sentimentalisation of both the land and heterosexual partnership which undermines its superficially happy close. The subsequent and more successful *The Camomile* sees Scotland, and specifically Glasgow, as a place from which a woman must flee if she is to find any kind of artistic self-realisation. ("A voice cries in my ear, 'This is not your world! Get out of this! Find your own place!' But where, what is my world?... Are not these the people I have grown up among? Why should their thoughts be so unfamiliar, even grotesque to me?"[8]) The end of Willa Muir's *Imagined Corners*, with its rich if perhaps unconscious lesbian resonances ("Well, my dear Elise, you have run away with her, you say? Have you then given up men?"[9]) carries the same message. Elizabeth and Elise, two women who read like different parts of the same person, and need to be with one another if they are to live with any authenticity, leave Calderwick for France, where they definitely will not meet up with Elise's non-Scottish husband. He has conveniently died (shades of *Villette*).

"Nationalism is always bad news for women." When an English academic made this pronouncement at a day seminar in St Andrews a year ago, I was not sure how to respond. Perhaps Carswell and Muir would have agreed with her. And the authority of Virginia Woolf's classic statement was hovering conveniently in the background. The woman had lived in Scotland for years, rearing a family and teaching a literature subject for much of that time. Her confession earlier to thorough ignorance of Scottish literature, calculated to disarm, came over as a barely disguised insult.

Being a man, it was hard for me to confront her with a defence of nationalism. I couldn't pretend that I knew what was good or bad for women. I could have come out to her as gay. Not all feminists, however, are sensitive to trifling distinctions of sexual orientation. The rejoinder I wanted to make was "You're just saying that because you're English." But she had played a trump card. After all, a watered-down feminism has become orthodoxy in academic and more generally 'culture-oriented' circles.

This is a phenomenon that, as a gay man, I observe from the sidelines with a certain wry amusement. It is instructive to note how rarely the personal conduct of male and female (heterosexual) colleagues bears out their enthusiastic mission statements, or how easily feminism combines with homophobia. The wryness extends to reading too. When the heroine of Janice Galloway's *The Trick is to Keep Breathing* describes shaving her legs to make herself more presentable to her male lover, I think I am supposed to be appalled. ("It gives a better finish slicing upward, against the hair; it doesn't catch or draw blood. That would be unsightly."[10]) Instead I just find it odd. After all, body hair is rarely a problem for gay men. From this particular perspective, many feminists appear overwhelmingly preoccupied with the heterosexual crisis: crisis of eroticism, crisis of roles, crisis of power and of relationships. I observe them rather as a convinced Scottish nationalist might observe the democratic crisis in the British (English) state, or a European Muslim the torments of a lapsed Catholic. It is more than my life is worth to ignore what is happening, since these people's conflicts affect me deeply. But they do not command my allegiance.

I am particularly wary of male colleagues who become energetic supporters of feminism. This is in part due to the 'I can do that too' syndrome. If men can read, teach and analyse women's texts as competently as women themselves, then there is no need for more women to be put in positions of cultural and academic power. The old guard can apply the same tools to the new agenda, recolonising the space women had opened up for themselves. It is as if men constantly felt the need to reply to women's discourse about women, to cap their statements.

The most pernicious effect of such beguiling liberalism may be unintended. Men who convert to feminism often do so to avoid ever articulating their own position. If all the talk is about women, masculinity can be kept securely out of the limelight. We are endlessly ready to talk about you because this will save us from ever having to talk about ourselves.

The televised 'essay' which Robert Crawford provided for STV's St Andrew's Day celebrations at the end of 1993 was highly instructive in this respect. The spectacle of Robert being ferried around what looked like Newton Mearns in the back of a taxi and in a manner vaguely reminiscent of royalty was not without its charms. But he was poorly served by his programme makers. The treatment of women was intriguing. When he declared the importance of giving women's writing its due place in the overall panorama of Scottish literature, his voice cut out. He was left still gesturing at his podium while, on the video screen to his right, a woman's lips began to mouth the words. We did see her face but she was consistently fetishised. Those watching naturally made the assumption that she was mouthing Robert's text, an even more peculiar phenomenon. Although he seemed to have passed the initiative to her, it was evident that he retained absolute control. The feminine lips were dummy to his ventriloquist.

This presentation was a splendid paradigm of the liberal attitude to minorities. (I can explore this paradigm without necessarily attributing all the attitudes to Robert Crawford). Those who hold power are perfectly willing to concede certain spaces to 'minorities' provided the reins of power remain firmly in their hands. So they can demonstrate their moral superiority and feel good about themselves without taking any genuine risks. (This is why the terms 'acceptance' and 'tolerance' are anathema to many gay men and lesbians. They imply that the moral majority will continue to dictate what is acceptable).

The programme implied that Crawford was ready to allocate a limited discursive space to women without questioning his own right to speak and be heard, or needing to examine the grounds on which space had been allocated to him. The central, empowered position aims to be axiomatic, invisible. We can assign any number of adjectives to it: white, male, heterosexual, middle-class, Protestant, academic. It does not have a distinctive voice because those who speak from there rarely see their own partiality. They are not different. They speak for humanity. Positions exist only as divergences from their own. The centre is not a position. It is not a place.

This was the effect of the scene, although none of it may have been intended by Crawford when he penned the 'essay'. My assumption that the disembodied lips were mouthing his words may even be unjustified, though I cannot help feeling that for Crawford to continue to speak in competition with an independent voice, the two trying to drown each other out, would have been a more accurate and honest paradigm of how power relations really work.

My own attitude is that much of the time women should just be left to get on with it. The soundest approach is for everyone to fight his or her own battles. The position we understand best is the one we find ourselves in. Operating from there it is possible to form a complex web of changing alliances depending on the issue at stake. The alliances would be based on contingency, on shared interests and on the acknowledgement of differences rather than polarities.

What I did was to ask if a Scottish woman wanted to comment. Even though it was an academic gathering in the east of Scotland, at least one woman present *was* Scottish. She disagreed with the Englishwoman, hesitantly but resolutely. Shared Scottishness brought men and women closer together in this country, she told us. At least, that was her experience.

So far I have presented gender, sexual orientation and nationality as interacting in problematic ways. Here was an example of a positive, enabling interaction between two categories. A Scottish woman might, under certain circumstances, feel closer to a Scottish man than to an English woman. (One consequence of gay and lesbian liberation and the increasing visibility of gay and lesbian people is that many (straight) men may feel they have more in common with a (straight) woman than with another (gay) man. Sexual orientation takes precedence over gender.)

The weakness of Virginia Woolf's position derives from its use of unwieldy categories such as 'women' and 'men' and its refusal to set gender distinctions in the context of a web of other, often equally important distinctions. It is increasingly hard to see the interests of all 'women' as ever being, in any situation, exactly the same. Moreover, Woolf was an Englishwoman. She belonged not only to the most successful Empire in modern history but to the most successfully imperialist literature western Christendom has so far seen. Access to her language and its literature may have been threatened by English men. Speakers and writers of another language belonging to a different national culture did not stand in her way.

And so the possibility emerges that a national culture such as Scotland's could, conceivably if not actually, be more receptive and more nurturing to women, gay men and other 'marginal' groups than larger, more dominant cultures. Bringing this about cannot be entrusted to the liberals. If a watered-down feminism has become the orthodoxy in establishment circles, this is a reaction to change rather than a way of initiating change.

It looks as if, in cultures such as Scotland's, a great deal of creative power is currently emanating from members of 'marginal' groups. Let me offer two examples, both taken from analogous cultures outside Scotland.

Mark Fisher's witty characterisation of the Quebec playwright Michel Tremblay as "the best playwright Scotland never had" has stuck. That Tremblay's work consistently matches, when it does not outclass, the best original theatre in Scots from Scotland is partly a tribute to his translators Martin Bowman and Bill Findlay. Audiences admired the splendid roles for an all female cast in *The Guid Sisters*, the careful delineation of three distinct registers of Scots in *The House Among the Stars* and the poignant analysis of family tragedy in *The Real World*. Each of these plays is a direct product of Tremblay's position as a gay man within a marginalised culture. He was certainly not imported into Scots primarily because of his gayness. But the gayness came across too because of its crucial role in enabling his human and linguistic achievement. It was part of the package.

Terenci Moix is perhaps the most successful of the group of Catalan novelists born in the 1940s and early 1950s. His particular form of betrayal has been to switch from writing in Catalan to writing in Spanish. Catalan literature, as seen from Barcelona, is literature in the Catalan language. However impressive the work of a man or woman born and bred in Barcelona, if it is written in Spanish, it is not part of Catalan literature.

In 1992 Moix published his first major Catalan text for many years, *El sexe dels angels* (The Sex of Angels), a novel he had worked on from 1969 to 1972 and then set aside. Its protagonist is a novelist with two names, Lleonard Pler and Jordi Lledó, who obtains sexual gratification through more and more extreme forms of masochism. He is thus, like his author, a sexual outsider, though one would hesitate to define him simply as gay.

One of Lleonard's more outrageous escapades is to photograph an egg with the Catalan flag balancing on top of a fountain of piss produced by a recumbent Japanese girl whose special turn this is. He puts the image of the dancing egg on his Christmas cards and is hauled up before a prominent banker, one of the renowned patriots who provide Catalan language culture with financial backing. (The novel is set during the Franco years). 'If you're so brave, why didn't you use the Spanish flag?' asks the banker. 'I couldn't give a damn about the Spanish flag,' answers Lleonard. 'It isn't mine. I can't even be bothered messing with it. But I love our flag more than my life, and that love gives me the right to shit on it if I want to.'[11]

For the respectable Catalan bourgeois Lleonard is a pervert and a renegade. But he insists that the symbols of the nation belong as much to him as they do to the unassailably powerful giant of finance.

The outsider, then, is not always an outsider, be he the fictitious novelist Pler or the real-life novelist Moix. "Exclusion is part of the game, but it is also a position in the game." The margins are not always on the periphery but can be where things really happen. How useful is it to carry on talking about margins in a culture that finds itself at this juncture? Does the centre retain a meaning to associate with its (possibly vestigial) power? Or do we have to find a completely new way of talking about what is happening?[12]

REFERENCES
1. Christopher Isherwood *Christopher and His Kind* (New York 1976) 159-162, 335-336. 2. Virginia Woolf *Three Guineas* (Penguin 1977: originally 1938) 122-125. 3. Neil Gunn *The Silver Darlings* (London 1969: originally 1941) 230. 4. William Soutar *Poems* (Edinburgh 1988) 226. 5. Hugh MacDiarmid Complete *Poems Vol.1* (London 1978) 114. 6. Ibid., 489. 7. Neil Gunn *Butcher's Broom* (London 1977: originally 1934) 9-10. 8. Catherine Carswell *The Camomile* (London 1987: originally 1922) 230. 9. Willa Muir *Imagined Corners* (Edinburgh 1987: originally 1931) 281. 10. Janice Galloway *The Trick is to Keep Breathing* (London 1991) 47. 11. Terenci Moix *Lleonard o el sexe dels angels* (Barcelona 1992) 365-370. 12. The sentence about exclusion is by Josep-Anton Fernández of Queen Mary & Westfield College, London. Katie Gramich of Trinity College, Carmarthen tells me that the Welsh word 'cenedl' means both 'nation, race' and '(grammatical) gender'.

Mary Montgomery

Fearg

Feumar aideachadh
Thug i fada feitheamh
A-mach tro na ficheadan
Cha do thog i ceann
Gus na fhàs i abaich
'S a dh'iarr i guth dhi fhèin
Cha robh for sa bith agam
Fiùs gu robh i ann
Gun deach fìrinn air a bonnan
An aghaidh fealla-dhà
'S a thàinig orm a frithealadh
An àit a dhol a ghàir
Ach dè seo bh' air a cùlaibh
Bha a feagal a bh' orm ro chàch
Gu faiceadh iad nach robh mi fìor
'S gu faigheadh iad cothrom tàir.
Bha mo chainnt òg easgaidh
Is duilich a cumail solt
Is ghabh mo chiad chànan
Ceum ri cùl mo chois
'S ged a dh'fheuch mi brodadh
A bhith sgiobalt luath
Ruith mi mach à fearg fo dheireadh
'S leigidh mi leatha bhith nis aig fois.

Anger

It must be admitted
It waited for long
Out through my twenties
It didn't lift its head
Until it matured
And claimed its own voice
I had no idea
It was even there
Until truth stood its ground
Against poking fun
And I had to attend to it
Instead of laughing it off
But what was behind it
Was fear that the others
Would see I wasn't true
And would scorn.
My young speech was keen
And hard to keep quiet
And my first language took
A step behind my heel
And though I tried to spur it
To be smart and fast
I eventually ran out of anger
And I'll now let it be at rest.

Tombas dè tha ceàrr

Tha cudthrom nam inntinn
Is faileas nam shùil
Mhùchadh mo dhòchas
Is bhriseadh mo dhùil
Lùbadh mo ghlùinean
Is leagadh mo cheann
Shcracadh mo phàipear
Is ghoideadh mo pheann
Tha ionndrainn nam anam
'S tha mo chridhe fo bhròn
Tha snaim air mo theanga
Is cnag air mo shròin

Guess what's wrong

There's a weight in my mind
And a shadow in my eye
My hope was suffocated
And my expectation broken
My knees were bent
And my head was bowed
My paper was torn
And my pen stolen
There's a want in my soul
And my heart is sad
There's a knot on my tongue
And a peg on my nose

Nach robh e math

Nach robh e math a bhith ri
    prògraman
'S a bhith gan clàradh còmh' ri càch
Do Ghaidheil bheaga bhrèagha òg
A' cheart cho math ri bhith ri
    bàrdachd
Air mo shocair fhìn
Do Ghaidheil ghlice chòire shean

Nach robh e math a bhith a'
    cruthachadh
Rud às an tigeadh feum
Beag no mòr a choireigin
Do chuideigin
Is rudeigin's dòch' a bha toirt tlachd
Dhan inntinn

'S far an robh mo thlachds' an sin
Tha beàrn mar bheàrn is fhiach a
    spreaghadh
Aig na h-oirean
Oir 's iad na h-oirean
Tha fada fad' ro chruaidh
Cho cruaidh ri creig
Nach gabh a leaghadh

Wasn't it good

Wasn't it good to be making
    programmes
And recording them with the others
For lovely little young Gaels
Just as good as making poetry
In my own quiet way
For wise and kind old Gaels

Wasn't it good to be creating
Something in which there was some
    use
Big or small
For someone
And something maybe that gave
    pleasure
To the mind

And where my pleasure lay in that
There is now a gap like a gap worth
    exploding
At the edges
Because the edges
Are far far too hard
As hard as rock
That will not take a melting

Gordon Meade

Cormorants in China

Tied up like dogs on leads,
Or tethered like farmyard goats
To munch their way around a circle of weeds,
Cormorants in China fish for men.

Diving down on lengths of twine,
They deliver what they find to waiting
Hands. Standing on the prows of boats, more
Beautiful than cockatoos, more fancied

Than our cloth-capped pigeons, less
Captive than our factory chickens, they're just
As used. You'll never see them banging on their
Bars like demented parrots. Their cages

Are invisible. I've seen them, majestic
In defeat, after a successful dive, hang out
The tattered banners of their flightless pride, as knives
Of greedy fishermen carve up their stolen prize.

Wild boar, May '92

At the risk of becoming one myself,
I want to talk about a 650lb wild boar,
Shot dead by an off-duty policeman

In Argyll, as it was rooting up raw
Potatoes, in a private garden in the village
Of St Catherines. Escaped from a wildlife park
In February, it swam two miles across Loch Fyne,
To be free. Now, another one's on the run,

In Perthshire, having jumped over the wall
Of an abattoir in Dunblane. When will it be
Tracked down, and slaughtered? For rooting up
Raw vegetables, with its hairy snout, in someone
Else's well-cultivated plot. For being,

A potentially dangerous animal,
Not kept in, behind bars, nor given
A uniform, or a rifle, but roaming free,
Through the remnants of its ancient woodland,
The broom and whin of Allan Water.

Whiting

Not really white, more olive green
On silver sand. A camouflage that's useless
Against a trawler's sonar, or its net's blind mesh,
Slipped around the fishes' necks and tightened.
Brought up into the light, their gloomy lives,
By dying, are somewhat brightened.

The smell of the fishmonger's slab
Hangs above the quay. Here the stench of death
Mingles with the freshness of countless lives drifting
Away. The only sounds are the incomprehensible words
Of the auctioneer. Like the fish, the bidders are
Silent, indicating their intentions

With the raising of an arm, the nod
Of a head, a knowing wink. An edible crab
Dislocates its dead mens' fingers in an enamel sink.
A dab flaps its weary tail on a bed of ice. Touch
The flesh of a cod, if you dare. All you will
Feel will be a skin made supple in water,

Stiffening in air. Taste its spoor off
Your fingers and savour the salt of the sea.
Leave that quay, with a shoal of images swimming in
Your head and try to haul up, from your own depths,
The flavour of a life, lived at the edge, and
Seasoned with the relish of death.

The Owl

Her face
Is a moon, a lamp
With wings,

Showing all the phases
That the waxing and the waning
Of her flying brings.

My face is the dial
Of a compass. My tongue, a needle,
Trying to point in all

Directions at once.
My speech, the pellet of a mouse,
Expelled from her mouth.

An Erotic Story

Rosalind Brackenbury

Somewhere at lunch the other day, the question came up about erotic writing, what it is; yes, it was in thinking about the Australian women's book of erotica, which I did not find very erotic. We faced each other across the little table, in the wine bar. What is it? The flavour, the spice is here, in this intensity of conversation, in the two wine glasses, the taste of smoked salmon. We are hunting it down like trained hounds after truffles. It is the taste of life, there in between the words, in what is not said. In paintings, it is sometimes the thickness of the paint, the way light is made to fall. It is not the thing itself, but the way it is seen.

One of us is talking about life, about a moment full of pain and pleasure. The other listens. The exact quality of the time, the flavour of it, is as tangible, as real as the sensation of smoked salmon, cut in thickish slices, breaking up between the palate and the tongue. We create with what we choose, what we exclude, eat and wear. Today, there is this rich mixture of writing, food, love, clothes. Every detail matters. We talk about the details, the cut of a sleeve, the fall of a neckline, the end of a sentence, the taste of a wine, the colour of things. You could say it is an intensely, typically female world. But we are ranging through it with the power of explorers, we have all the equipment, the tools, the experience. We are not dabbling, but going right in there, going deep.

We meet, often, in the times between publications, between love affairs, between meetings of importance, between encounters. We talk about our work. Our work is the visible tip of this vast, shifting mass, this land mass that is life. Today, I have a sense of excitement. I see you come in through the door of the wine bar, dressed in black, with a flicking back of your hair, and I have this sense of relish, of what we will talk about, what we will do.

The erotic story could be about two women meeting at lunchtime in a wine bar and drinking some strong, dark Australian wine that they ordered by mistake, that stings the backs of their throats like a salt wave and that does not go with the smoked salmon except in the basic way that fish goes with the salt wave and blistering sun goes with the grit of sand and then with the balm of smoothed-on oil. You put two differing things together, and see what happens. It is never predictable. Outside, the day is sometimes sunny and sometimes grey. It is a day of shifting, variable things, no strong sunlight that stripes everything into brilliance and shade, none of the take-it-or-leave-it of absolutes, of sexual encounters. Perhaps the erotic happens in between, hides between the states of pure sensuality, flickers beneath covers, wears layers and leaves, will not be easily defined.

Before I got here, I was with my lover; this for me is the day after, when I have not yet collected myself together, I am still vague and a bit lost. After you leave, you will go to a phone box and dial the number of a man you love, whom you had intended to leave. You will meet him, in this exact place, but downstairs, in the basement, where it is possible to sit undisturbed, for hours. In between, we weave a world which includes the before and the after, the men who are not here but who have touched or will touch us, a world in which all is to be alchemically transformed, magically recreated, presented back to the real world, the world of readers and critics and publishing and applause. Now, we are like actors, behind the scenes. We have not yet shown all this, not yet dared come out on to the stage and be seen, and risk being this naked and take it all, blame and applause and catcalls and acclaim, whatever comes our way. We will set off, once we have eaten and drunk and talked and woven all this into the rich text that it will possibly be, to find our costumes. We will buy clothes for the women we are to be tomorrow, the women who live all this, write all this, and appear, and are seen. We will try on and discard many garments: the severe and the frivolous, the revealing and the plain, clothes for being serious, clothes for being sensual, clothes for celibacy and clothes for lust. We will finger textures and essences. Silk, for what falls away purely and in one gesture, slipping to the floor at a touch. Tiny buttons, in rows, for being done up or loosed from their tiny sewn button holes, one by one, by a patient hand. The heavy fall of a coat to be wrapped around, to conceal, and then to open, in one casual gesture. Transparent materials, fine enough for babies; heavy, down-dropping silks like crêpe de chine; suedes to be marked by the touch of a finger; fine cottons to be crumpled in a hand. The material says it all: in this, I am untouchable, aloof, or, in this I am available – look, one hook and there, it falls away. We will walk before mirrors, absorbed in the sensations, the images, what we can create. We will invent people for each other to be: look, this could be you, tomorrow, from now on. We make up characters, and try them on, and leave them lying about on the changing room floor. The woman who keeps the shop will join in the game, in the story. She knows she has to, in order for her shop, her creation to work. She is in the story. She hands us the clothes, provides the narrative, keeps us going on from one thing to the next, handing the props, prompting the dialogues. In a sense, she is an editor, always encouraging us to go on.

– Is this me? Is this the me I am not yet, but am about to become? You are in front of the mirror, in white silk with your hair down your back, and the openness of the question does not alarm her. She knows better than to answer. She smiles, says something neutral. She is aware of process and limitation of words. She deals in essences, the materials, the things themselves. You are asking questions, before the mirror, about your power both as lover and writer, your power to choose.

What I am trying on is a blouse in which I will go to the launch of the book about women's writing by a feminist publishing house, but which expresses the longing to flaunt, to celebrate my body, which I have today. It is both severe and revealing. It excites me to see myself wear it, in the mirror; it is the extension of myself that I want, its statement at once serious, expensive, adult, and mischievous. It is the perfect blouse for today. Thinking of it, I will be able to write my erotic story. Even with it hanging in the wardrobe I will be on my way.

Of course, says the censor, this is all very self-indulgent, this stuff about smoked salmon and white silk and low necklines and the right wine. Can you not write without all this? Surely, life is about other things than this? And how can you, with your talk of lovers and fast cars and travel and clothes possibly connect with the woman of today, who is at work, not enjoying herself trapped in her kitchen?

I don't know; but have given up trying to justify, to explain, ultimately, to hide. The erotic, I think, is closer to the dream, to the secret, than to the fact out there in the light of day. And women are not allowed to bring out their secrets, live their dreams. We, you and I, are in the business of allowing this, as the woman in the clothes shop allows it. Look, try this, you will look good in it. Try a little dreaming. Try a little life.

We sat in another restaurant, he and I, and the dream was different, the story was different, but afterwards I thought, what we are and what we do creates what happens around us, sets the scene. We had just got out of bed, and come here. I do not know whether it was because this was so obvious that the manageress kept laughing, and trying to persuade us to go downstairs and sit in the restaurant where we would have peace and quiet. What do you do with a couple that has only just got out of bed and is spreading this mischief, this anarchy in the world? When they walk into your restaurant and order the same thing three times over, contradict themselves, want wine and water and drink out of the wrong glasses; when they do not feel quite properly dressed, when she has not even bothered to do her hair, when they are so hungry that they eat a whole basketful of bread? When what happens is that you end up giving their bill to the people at the next table, and nobody seems to mind and the people at the next table start flirting with the people who have only just got out of bed. They ask for the music to be turned down so that they can talk, and then all they do is kiss each other, and you wish to God, to simplify things, they would act their age, and just go down and be out of sight in the basement? In this restaurant, in this story, the erotic is potential chaos, confusion

At the time, I thought – what a chaotic restaurant. Now, I think – what effect were we having, he and I and our so-recent and evident love-making, upon the general scene? Or had everybody there spent their afternoon the way we had, bathed in the strong, hot, absolute light of sexual satisfaction? The wine came, the food came, and we all ate with the dedicated greediness of hungry children. I remember the lean black man with the Rasta hairdo at the bar, grinning at me as I dismembered my fish. The long-haired woman in the black velvet dress leaned over us like a nanny, flashing her ring and necklace, rearranging things, possibly just to be close to us: I with my vagueness and messy hair, he with his recognisable fed-cat look, his gleam. The music grew louder. We stopped bothering to talk, and touched feet under the table. The other people in the bar were all young, much younger than us, and many of them black and elegant, and others wore black and had outrageous hairstyles, and the Saturday night alcohol was slipping down, and there was this atmosphere of permissive friendliness that is unusual, that makes this part of a story. We went out into the night, and it was still light, with the trees of London growing heavy, and dark. We sat in his car and touched, to remember. There was a lightness about everything, as if everything in the world had lost weight, lost gravity. The power of sex moves from the inside, out into the world, it lingers, changing the way things are, changing atmospheres, changing the weight of things; juggling, making what is serious, light, what is light, real. We become unconscious of what we are doing, who we are, and move instinctively, and slower than usual, as if to allow life to catch up.

And what happens to the everyday things, the objects among which we live, when you are in this state? If life, and other people, appear to be making up an impromptu carnival for your benefit, and the world is a riot of colour and scents, and the dust and elderflower of summer London fill your nostrils more strongly than ever they did twenty, twenty-five years ago, and you feel the strong pulse of life beating with a regularity and persistence that carries you, so that you do not have to do a thing? The erotic is in chaos, in the tangled sheets on a bed, in clothes thrown about, in bread torn up with the teeth out of sheer hunger; it is also in the coolness of order, the knowing what comes next. I look into cupboards full of folded linen, wardrobes with shirts hanging in them, a new white curve of soap in a soapdish, shoes in a row, bottles in a rack. It is in what is not yet touched, not yet opened, not yet begun on. We make a bed with clean sheets, like turning the pages of a new book, and the fine, clean cotton is smooth to our fingers, reminding. This is a bed we will not lie in. These are the clean end-papers of the book, after the story has been told. Now, my mark has to be elsewhere. I take the blank, clean, white sheets of paper and begin. The erotic is in transformations of endings into beginnings, transposed, sung in a different key. I make the bed, and leave the room. Elsewhere, I take up white paper. There will be an end to this, too. Again, the marks will end. What will continue will take place in the eye and the mind of another. Together, we will stand in front of mirrors, and look. One story will meet up with another. The erotic runs underground, like secret rivers, and comes up in another place.

You know what I mean? This is the current of life, the one that is supposed not to exist. This is the one that women know about, and will not mention. Here be dragons. Dangerous, because they transform, or can transform, everything that they touch. A linen cupboard is no longer just a linen cupboard. Shopping is no longer shopping. A meal is not just eating. Even a piece of soap, lying so neatly in a curved soapdish the shape of a hand, will not be just itself. Things fit too closely, threaten to become each other. Whose is which, and where are the boundaries? Where do you end and I begin, whose is this experience, what are we doing together, what will it become?

The most powerful, and the most dangerous people, alchemists: turning what was seen as base metal into what was to be pure gold. Of course, they were only scientists, and scientists do it all the time. As do novelists. And we are only novelists. Sometimes, we meet for lunch.

Hugh Macpherson

Lovers and Unicorns

Lovers find squirrels to admire
in rain riven parks, and slip away
from offices and the demands of telephones,
their pockets crammed with broken nuts
to hold out to beasts that come without fear,
unicorn-like, from urban shrubberies that others find
deserted – while the city noise circles and roars
but doesn't dare come near.

Administrators, their own years of belief
behind them, watch with traditional envy,
fingering the curtains with impatience,
knowing reproaches are unacceptable and make
no difference, following the unravelling of events
with calculation, seeing easily a time when
no beasts come to beckoning hand, and business turns
to an escape from sharing that's got intense.

They can afford to wait: lack of faith
presents itself always as unarguable fate
– a park that chances to have no squirrels,
an apology that comes too grudgingly or late –
but the two emerging from today's glistening mists
know (today at least) that any place provides
the heraldic beasts of love in some form. It's never they
who leave reality but us, who are dismissed.

Telling Oneself It's Alright

I woke full of fears,
my hands locked in the claws of twisted bedclothes,
the soft sheets of only hours ago
now unforgiving strands of hard cloth
tightened round me.
Last night's silence that lay comfortably
clasped within the doors of every room
had left, the slow unwinking eye
of fridge in darkened kitchen changed to
a stark jaundiced gaze that had stared out all night.

It's too easy a pathos
to listen to morning rain and call
the world so difficult, too general
a self pity to indulge. Turn on the radio news

for company: the old reassurances are best.
But then truly the disasters begin:
children who can't reply to calls of help
in earthquake cities because their mouths will
fill with mud if they shout out,
the loveliest things crushed out of spite.

Just to keep sane then
we must forget the real, persuade ourselves
with probabilities of "not always" and "even if".
We fight off the knowledge of what we can't prevent.
But we still see how open to fate is every person
walking home with not unreasonable happiness,
each child with favourite bear.
But when we see how little this counts:
how easy to take the "realistic" view – the one
that's quite indifferent – or wake full of useless tears.

Duties

Each morning we ignored the sunlight
and drove down to the waterfronted
headquarters of official meetings,
its site surrounded by walls through which
we were admitted by guards,
recording details on clipboards
as we passed in. Prisoners of our process,
through limousine windows we would catch
a snatched perspective of promenaders
squinting against a wind that scuffed
at every breaker, and gave a ragged shape to pelicans
slowly gliding to a stop above the waves,
sinking as tired hovercraft on
the restful skirt of their feathers.
Frigate birds, their throats
swelled in bulbous scanners
of a bird borne radar force,
scrutinised submarine shoals and
the shift of ritual colours in the sea.
Birds and idlers, they shared duties
we had abandoned, telling the changes of creation
through each countdown minute of the day,
keeping scrupulous account of light and flow
while we, in isolation, exchanged details
of armed artifice, drove harder bargains
than we knew.

Iain Galbraith

Pan

He brushed the damp moss off his coat and ran;
he found streets where the walls bent narrow;
slickster, he joined the gang, fell in breaking bones.

He was the one they woke in the wood;
he used a goat path and gave them the slip;
he hooted at the tall sun over the first homes.

He rustled in the grass and the dogs caught on;
he was the quick hand behind the ribbed glass door;
stark pink in the porch-light, he clicked the night-lock shut.

His sap burned in the pines at the edge of town;
he flew through windows, licked front room ceilings,
got to know his way round paint and blades.

He was the one standing by the high copse;
he took kids to the derelict house,
pulled them up stone steps into cold kitchens.

He lay big-eyed under the fireflies;
he sidled up close in a sticky bar;
he had the loving-cup pressed to his lips.

His heart got crushed in the forester's tending hand;
he strode in and smashed the stained glass saints,
grabbed the pheremone, set to work with phials.

He knew well where the old town lay in ruins;
he peeled the notes off, got men running,
flashed on the screens, stammered out the pace.

He began to lose his way; he stepped
on the slug; he climbed the hill; he heard
the dogs, saw the lights, started to shout.

Sleep Talk

Along the sea-wall, houses listen,
their held breath shaped to bell-talk
with the lighter sky. Feelers on black roofs
touch pink tracks in the certain blue.

Dunlin swing in low over mudflats,
the swarm's one mind transparent
as they turn. Inland, cottonwoods
whitewash pavements with their summer snow.

Heard through blinds, a dreamer's tongue
is the hand that sounds the bell,
joins the blue. Working the tide,
it heaves back choices for the stony beach.

Wingdust

for Deborah Korner

In the window part of the moon
pokes out of the crumpled sky
like half a button. Everything
tonight was bent on lying down flat

to earth. Running feet pattered home
like a child's in the wet street —
voices that came had no throw,
sounds tumbled headlong in the grass.

Space filled up
with the rattle of a moth,
a circular career
magnified through a thin screen.

Memory touched
leaves wingdust on our fingers.

Prison Letters

April
It is absence
of light
that pains,
of sound.

Let this page
be a tunnel
through the table's brotherly wood.

Let me hear
the wryneck call
among orchard buds.

June
I dreamt of a place,
a place called Corse,
a woman's round belly
beneath a stone arch.

I dreamt of Time,
our hope sent
sprawling under the yoke.

I rose
wanting the air.
The woman's wet pink face
was crossed with veins.

August
Your letter
lies folded on my bed.
I had to weep
for the dying songbirds.

Walking the walls in the heat
I think of men under trees
heaping cherries
into wide baskets.

September
Here is my body's hand,
spent,
weighing on my mind.

October
Brambles
behind empty pigsties
sway in the rising wind.

The sky has broken.
The people leave
their wooden shacks.

I could not move.
I gripped the bars
with both my hands.

December
is memory now –
waters and blood
on the woman's thighs.

The Collogue o the Birdies

Sheena Blackhall

Aroon the time o Beltane, in Weirdich Wid, bi the derk, cauld, tod-hauntit Lochan o Mortlich, awa at the Back o Beyont, the Bard o the birdies deed, the coo's lick peesie. Sae the birdies summoned Murdoch, the hoodie craw, tae dae the beeryin. Bit there wis nae bard tae cry the coranach ower the corp, or reeze oot his lifetime's wirth, nur yet tae soun his name an the name o his forebears aroon the Howe! The birdies war gey sair-made aboot the plyter they fand thirsels in, till a wee yalla yeitie hoppit forrit.

"We maun haud a collogue o the birdies tae wyle a new bard frae wir mids'", she tweetled. "An as Calum the hoolet is weel kent fur his wyceness, we maun speir gin he'll agree tae be judge ower aa." Sae the birdies flew tae the mids o Weirdich Wid, far Calum the hoolet bedd in the intimmers o an auld wheezy aik, tae sikk his answer.

Calum the hoolit sleepit aa throw the day, sae they'd a gey tcyauve tae wauken him, bit efter a skreich frae Murdoch the hoodie craw in his lug, the muckle hoolet steered, an drew his hairt-shapit heid frae his breist. "Fit brings aabody here tae ma door in sikk a steer?" he winted tae ken. "Peesie the Bard o the birdies his deed, an we maun wyle anither Bard frae wir mids", quo the yalla yeitie. "We hae cam tae sikk yer guid offices, as judge o wir collogue."

"First," the hoolet said, "ye maun send wird tae the birdies that their presence is socht here this day."

Sae, far an wide aroon the Howe, the yeitie sent meesengers bearin invites tae atten the birdies' collogue, fur tae chuse a Bard. Tae the north flew the whaup, far the muckle Bens war cled wi snaa, an the pine an fir staun sentry ower the burns. He brocht back Padraig the ptarmigan, frae his heddery hame. Tearlach the erne frae the broo o a steep cliff, an Feinn, the capercaillie, the auld man o the wids, frae the foun o a michty fir. Tae the sooth, flew Magnus the magpie, tae the lochan o Mortlich itsel, far shrubs an rowan an elder, beech an birk an whin grew thick aroon. An Magnus brocht back Malcolm the merle, frae a neuk o twisted breem, wee Willie Wagtail frae a clump o seggs at the lochan's rim, an Ginty the gowk, frae her brakkfast o hairy caterpillar unner a beech tree's reets. Tae the east, wi a saft breeze, flew Malloch the mavis, far an eildritch ruined kirk wis beeriet deep in the mids o Weirdich wid. An he brocht back Grigor the pheasant, frae a park o breirin barley thereaboots, an Seonaid the swallaa, frae her nest neth the auld kirk bell, an Witter the warbler frae her cosie hame in the girsse in the green kirkyaird.

Hinmast ava, tae the wast o the wid, tae the stoory toun that wis thrang wi fowk, flew the wee Robin reidbriest. An he brocht back Teenie Ann the spurgie, frae the back o a soutar's drainpipe, Drochle the doo frae the cassies aneth a railin, an the wee Jennie wren, frae her hoosie o hair, an moss an feathers, far her wee cheepers war yet tae be born.

Fin aa the winged fowk o the air war settled on their reists aroon the hoolet's hame, the yalla yeitie swalled her breist wi win. "Chi-chi-chi-chi-chi-chi-chi-cheeee", she skreiched. "We are gaithered thegither this day tae chuse a new Bard for the birdies, an Calum the hoolet will help us decide, fur he is the wycest bird in Weirdich wid."

"Tsp tsp", cried the wee Robin reidbreist. "This'll nae hinner lang. Aabody kens fit makks a blythe bardie. He maun be douce, an couthie, an cantie. He maun rhyme like the watter rinnin in the burn. His vyce maun be hinney on the lug, tae saften the hairt, bring a tear tae the ee, an a smile tae the moo. Yon's fit gyangs tae makk a blythe bard."

"Faith ay", quo Teenie Ann, the spurgie. "A Bardie maun spikk fur aa the winged fowk, an nae a twa three rarifeed peacocks roond the laird's hoose. Rhyme an lilt an douceness, like the Ettrick Shepherd or Burns, thon are the merks o a bard."

"Agreed", tweetled the teenie-weenie Jenny wren. "An sae the verra bird tae be the birdies' bard is Drochle the cushie doo. Her curmurrin saftens the hairt, brings a smile tae the moo an a tear tae the ee betimes." Sae the yeitie an the hoolet bad the doo step forrit, tae see fit she cud dae.

"Curdoo, curdoo", sang Drochle the doo as she cleared the rochle frae her thrapple. An syne, she rhymed a rhyme that telt o the bonnie reemin burns o auld Scotia, till ye cud near hear the waves lowp in yer lug. An she rhymed a rhyme that fuspered o the win amang the barley, till ye cud hear the gowden heids o corn jig jiggin wi the simmer breeze.

"Man, yon wis bonnie", quo the yalla yeitie. "There's nane can rhyme sae free's the cushie doo."

Bit, Calum the hoolit thocht, that tho rhyme an soun war gran an fine an musical as a bardie's wirds sud be, he widna jist lowp at the first flech, as the auld troots say, bit wad wyte till he'd seen aa the flechs a-steerin.

"Fit think *ye* makks a guid bard?" speired the hoolet o the magpie, Magnus. Noo Magnus wis a kenspeckle craitur fa gaithered nippicks o news frae aa the airts. He likit glittry gee-gaws an aa mainner o glamourie.

"A Bardie maun reel oot a praise poem fur chiefs, an heroes, an bonnie weemin", quo he. "He maun spikk o luv an coortin. Bit mair nur yon, ye maun aye be wullin tae wyle mair lear frae the fower neuks o the warld… fur a cock that craws anely on the heid o its ain midden, is naethin bit an aiblich efter aa, a nochtie body o smaa accoont. Sae I coonsel ye tae speir mair o ma fiers, Willie Wagtail, an Malcolm the merle, nae forgettin Ginty the gowk, fur ye sud ay be open tae anither's thochts."

Syne forrit bobbit Willie Wagtail, his sark like a penguin's dickie an his wee tail jinkin up an doon like a kangaroo. "Chizick, chizick", cried he. "I hae wintered in Cadaqués, in Spain, bi the hame o a peinter chiel caad Dali, an learned muckle o the wirkins o the Muse, fa veesits poets, peinters, an singers alike."

"An fit learned ye there?" speired Magnus, cockin his heid ajee.

"Weel, Dali swackened his harns bi glowerin at the clouds, the rocks, or the san, tae imagine aa mainner o ferlies therein, a kinno dwaumin like the great peinter Leonardo da Vinci coonselled his students tae dae. Ye'll fin the marra o't, in Shakespeare's Hamlet, fin the prince deaves Polonius:

The Collogue o' the Birdies

"Painting is Mute
Poetry, & Poetry a
Speaking Picture"
(Simonides)

S. Blackhall

Hamlet: D'ye see yon cloud that's gey like a camel?
Polonius: By Certes, it's fair like a camel.
Hamlet: It minds me o a futterat.
Polonius: Ay, it's humfy like a spittan futterat.
Hamlet: Or mebbe like a whale?
Polonius: Unca… like a whale.[1]

"An fit mair learned ye frae this Dali chiel?" speired Magnus.

"Weel, he trawled his harns fur thochts, doon tae the verra founs o his kennin, doon intae the subconscious itsel. He made eese o his dwaums in his wark. Near aa the poets an peinters aroon the Mediterranean hae steepit thirsels in the buiks o Freud, y'unnerstaun. Dali hissel pit it this wye: 'Tae ken foo tae luik at a ferlie or a breet through thocht, is tae luik wi the maist pouerfu reality. Bit fowk see anely stereotyped picturs o aathin teem o meanin, an ferlies they see ilkie day they caa common. They hae *tint the mystery o the ordinar.*'[2] Fin I wis bidin in Dali's airt, a frien cried inby, a French Surrealist poet bi the name o André Breton. He pit it this wye: 'Aathin gars us ken that at ae pynt in the mind, life an daith, the real an the dwaum, ahin an efter, the spikkable an its contrar, the heich an the laigh, are nae langer set ane agin the ither …duality's connached.'"[3]

At this up bobbit the merle, fa's vyce wis douce an bonnie's a flute. "I hae bidden in Belgium aa winter," quo he, "an fit wagtail says is true. I warmed masel aneth the lee o the biggin o a peinter caad René Magritte, an he hid muckle tae say aboot creativity, fur withoot thon spirk frae the muse, aa picturs, poems an sangs are cauld kail hett again.

"'The first darg o peintin, is tae makk poetry veesible', quo Magritte. 'Tak fur instance, a tree. It grows frae the yird tae the sun, an image o blythe-ness. Tae tak tent o this image, we maun staun as still's the tree. Gin we meeve, tis the tree that's luikin at us. It bides in the shape o cheers, brods, an yetts, watchin the shiftin spectacle o wir life. Syne the tree becams a kist an is beeriet in the grun. Fin it's kinnelt, it mells wi the air.'"[4]

"A gey wyce chiel, Magritte", quo the Magpie. "Did ye learn ony mair?"

"Oh ay, I heard him say this", quo the bird: "'The picturs maun be seen fur thirsels. My picturs dinna heist the veesible ower the inveesible …the letter happit in the envelope isna veesible, bit it's there jist the same. The mind lues the unkent. It lues picturs fas meanins are unkent, sin the meanin o mind itsel is unkent. The mind disna unnerstaun its ain raison d'être, an wioot unnerstaunin yon, the puzzles hae nae rizzon either.'"[5]

"A gey far-seein chiel, richt eneuch", quo the hoolet. "Wis yon aa yer lear frae the Belgian mannie?"

"We'd be here aa day an hauf o the morn, an I wadna hae scrattit the tap o't", quo the merle. "Here's anither spikk he wis fond o: 'Fowk wint somethin tae lean on sae they can be comfy. They wint somethin tae haud ontil, tae save them frae the void. Fowk faa luik fur symbolic meanins in aathin, tyne the pouer an mystery the image hauds inbye itsel.'[6]

"'In ma bairnhood,' Magritte wad say, 'I eesed tae play wi a quinie in an auld rick-ma-rick o a kirkyaird, in a kintra toun far I bedd ma holidays. We'd heist up the iron yetts an gyang doon unnergrun tae the vaults. Climmin up tae the licht ae day, I fan in the mids o some brukken steen columns an tapsalteerie leaves, a peinter come frae the capital, fa seemed tae me as a bairn tae be wirkin magic. Fin I sterted tae peint, the thocht o yon first eildritch trysts wi peintin held me forrit …I thocht that I cud hae the warld I lued in ma pouer forever an ay, gin I catched its marra on canvas'"[7]

At this, the gowk lowpit up an doon in a birr. "Cuckoo, cuckoo", she cried. "Yon's richt, as sure's be here. Aa the lang winter, I bedd in the hairt o Afric, i the reef o a warlock's shiel. He wis bard, an physeecian, an meenister, tae the derk-skinned fowk o the birsslin hett sun. HE wad tell ye the pouer o the pictur, an the pouer o the spukken wird. Gin he'd makk a rhyme, twis fur guid or evil …I hae seen a hairty chiel sicken an dee in a meenit, wi twa three wirds frae his mou …an gin he vrocht a likeness o ain o his tribe, they wauked in fear, kennin he'd catched their soul."

"We sikk nae bard wi frichtsome pouers like yon", quo the yalla yeitie. "The Druids are deid an beeried in this kintra, an lang may they bide deed."

"Haud wheesht fur the mavis", cried the hoolet. "He maun step forrit noo wi his fower fiers. Makk wye fur Malloch the mavis."

Malloch the mavis hoppit doon frae his reest, dandy in his broon an cream jaiket, an at his back sprang doon the swalla, the warbler an the pheasant, trailin his lang glimmrin train o a tail.

"As some here niver weary tellin me", quo Grigor the pheasant, "I'm jist an incomer tae Scotia, taen ower frae Asia bi the Romans, an lat wanner lowse in yer lan. Bit I've bidden here as lang's the Celts, sae hae earned the richt tae be caad a Scot, an nae a broon settler, as some o ye cheep ahin ma back. Fur fit it's wirth, I aften traivel aroon the gruns o a muckle hoose aa its lane nearhaun the barley park. In yonder, there bides fowk faas harns an hairts hae bin bladdit bi the weird they've dreed. Chiels caad psychiatrists luik efter them. Inby yon muckle hoose, whyles ye'll see patients peintin an screivin. They tell me the darg's caad Psychosynthesis, makkin eese o guided fantasy … garrin them regain control o thirsels an their warld. Fur bladdit bairns, there's nae ither wye whyles, tae unlock fit's inby their hurtit briests an heids. Mebbe yon's fit a bard dis … pits us back in touch wi wir ain deepest thochts an feelins…"

Malloch the mavis cleared his thrapple an dichtit his neb, sittin squar on his hunkers. "I hae wintered in Asia, an learned muckle o eese. Tae sherpen yer thocht ye maun bide in the leevin meenit. It braks the bubble that separates watcher an watched …it kens naethin o self'. The Buddha telt a parable in a sutra. A chiel traivellin ower a park spied a tiger chasin him. He ran tae a cliff, catched haud o a rowan reet an flang hissel ower the tap. The tiger snochered abeen him. Trimmlin, the chiel luikit doon. Aneth, anither tiger wis wytin tae ett him, doon at the cliff foun. Anely the rowan keepit him safe. Twa moosies, ain fite, ain blaik, sterted tae chaw the rowan reet. The chiel spied a sappy reid straaberry growin aside him. Grippin the rowan wi ae haun, he puued the berry wi the ither. Foo swete it tasted!"[8]

"The pheasant fowk hae a legend haundit doon frae Basho, the great bard", quo Grigor the pheasant. "'Gyang tae the pine' (quo Basho) 'gin ye wint tae learn aboot the pine. An leave aa yer thochts aboot yer ainsel ahin, or ye'll niver learn onythin. Poetry cams unsocht *fin ye've melled wi the pine* ... fin yer mind an ee an hairt hae breenged forrit deep inno the pine tae catch somethin glimmrin there. Gin the pine an yersel bide separate, ye'll *niver* be a bard.'[9] 'Stop the watter, an grip the burn. Haud the air, an ain the lift. Sic a glekit tcyaave! Tae ain the lift, becam the lift. Tae ain the watter becam the watter.'[10]

"The mavis his bin byordnar quate", quo the yalla yeitie. "Is he sleepin?"

"Na faith", leuch Grigor the pheasant. "He is watchin his braith, slaw an siccar, cairryin life an prana frae the air tae his briest. He is quatenin his thochts."

"A queer-like plavver", quo the hoolet, mystifeed. "Tell's mair."

Syne the warbler bobbit forrit. "I hae wintered in Afric," quo he, "in the hame o an Indian swami fa bedd in a Buddhist clachan there. The mavis is calmin his body, afore he meditates, jist like humans pit on their dookers afore they dook."

"Fit's an Indian swami daein bidin in Afric?" speired Teenie Ann the spurgie.

"Fit's a Chinee pheasant daein in Scotia!" cam the warbler's repon. "As I wis sayin. Ae thing the swami did wis jist tae luik at ferlies. 'The peinter an poet learn tae luik at a tree, or a physog, or a vase o flouer. A mind that's trained like yon grows inno a guid tool fur the eese o its maker. Bit cannie ... tho the rider o the shelt micht think hissel onno the breet's back, the shelt will aye try tae cowp him aff. His students canna unnerstaun foo concentration is said tae be hard, till the swami tells them tae glower fur five meenits at a doorknob wioot ony ither thochts lowpin up ither than the thocht o the doorknob. The mind seen scunners at the doorknob. It disna like the doorknob. It gets nae pleisur ooto watchin a doorknob.'"[11]

"Ye'll ken the Chinee tale o the twa monks", broke in the pheasant. "They argie-bargied aboot a flag blawn in the win. 'It's the flag that meeves', quo the first. 'It's the wind that meeves', quo his fier. 'It's neither that meeves,' quo their maister, 'anely the mind itsel.' Fowk in the wast craw aboot *maisterin* Nature. Fowk in the east are in pairtnership wi Nature. As Li Po, Cheena's graitest bard aince screived, 'We niver grow weariet o ain anither, the Ben an me.'"[12]

Malloch the mavis, wis dowpit doon, incantin wirdies ower an ower. "He's recitin a mantra", quo the pheasant. "It's weel kent wirds hae the power tae quaten the mind."

"AND images", butted in the merle, minin upon Magritte.

The mavis opened his ee, an began tae spik.

"Patanjali, the faither o yoga, tells o the echt limbs o yoga. Abstinences (*yamas*), observances (*niyamas*), postures (*asanas*), braith control (*pranayama*) sense withdraal (*pratyabara*), concentration (*dharana*), meditation (*dhyana*), and contemplation (*samadhi*). The first twa are consarned wi the ethical purity o yoga, the neist twa wi physical purity, an the hinmaist fower are consarned wi tamin the mind, an kennin man's true Natur. Richt sittin, an richt braithin, pave the wye fur richt thinkin. Thocht can be as nerra or as braid's the reenge o a grand pianie. Aabody sud strive tae makk eese o as mony octaves as they can."[13]

"In concentration, the mind maun first be preened tae ae ferlie. In meditation, the mind dwalls on that ae ferlie, sookin up ilkie thocht it can, adee wi it. Hinmaist ava is contemplation ... the ferlie glimmers inbye wir teemed sel – the state of *samadhi*."[14]

Seonaid the swalla drappit doon aside the lave o the birdies. "I hae wintered in Afric anna," quo she, "an I hae veesited the tents o the Sufis. Ae day a pedlar cried inby their camp, frae Hindustan. He claiked aboot meditation anna. Quo he, 'The maist important darg, is practice. The mind jinks aboot like a monkey. It's aywis chappin at the yetts o the hairt, tae steer it up. Bit as mony times as the mind comes chappin tae pit ye in a tirrivee, chase it awa, an fix yer thochts on somethin o *yer* chusin!'"[15]

"Sae a guid bard, ye think, maun be an Eastern philosopher as weel's a poet..." quo the hoolet.

Oot lowped the yalla yeitie frae the mids o the collogue. "We hinna yet heard frae the birds o the North, fit they wad sikk in a bard. Step forrit the whaup, the ptarmigan, ern, an capercaillie!"

First forrit wis the auld man o the wids, Feinn, the capercaillie. "Tik-up, tik-up, tik-up", cried he, like a gun firin pellets inno a dyke. His reid ee flashed an his blaik tail spread like a fan as he gurred an whirred his wings in rooze at the lave o the winged fowk there.

"Maist o ye reestin here are fair-weather friens – 'fite settlers' an naethin mair. Ye traivel here fur the Simmer's pickins. Bit me an my kind bide here hear in year oot, thole aa an bide throw aa. An tae ye aa, I say, 'aa progress maun come frae deep inbye an canna be forced or hashed forrit bi ony short cuts; aathing is fermentation, like the barley bree – even thocht. Ilkie impression an nippick o feelin maun grow itsel in the derk, in the founs o kennin ayont the licht o the mind until the oor o its birth. That alane is the artists' life: in unnerstaunin as weel as creatin.'"[16]

"Faith", quo Tearlach the ern. "The auncient philosopher Horace spakk weel fin he said that the makkin o a poem is like a peintin. Fur aathin in life's a pictur, an wirds are bit scrats o letters haudin picturs, as I wi ma gleg ee can sweir tae. Heich in the lift far I bide, the warld is ae muckle pictur, an the burns an Bens bit patterns upon it – a poetry o silence an image."

Padraig the ptarmigan hirplit forrit. "Bit fit *is* imagination?" he spéired. "Is't fantasy – a thing *ye* will, or is't inspiration – a thing that comes fin *it* will? Is a bard born, or can a bard learn the trade? The druids hid twinty year apprenticeship afore aa their secrets war learned bi wird o mou. Is barderie a wye o luikin, or a wye o thinkin? Is't wirds, or souns, or picturs, or feelins, or a hotch potch o them aa in a bardic cauldron?"

At yon, the whaup steppit up. "True poetry his dule an wae in it, the greet o a lament, the grue o the forhooied, the hint o daith an the eildritch, the itherwarldly. Oor Gaelic bards wad tell ye there's mair o dule an gloam in guid Scots bardrie than iver there is o mirth. It maun gar ye greet an grue."

"Havers", argied the spurgie. "It maun set a glint in the ee an a lowp in the step. It maun be blythe an gleg as a wee hairst moosie. It maun gar ye lauch like the claas o an auld haimmer."

"Ay", quo the robin. "An it maun skinkle like frost ower watter. It maun be fey an fine, an spikk tae us o freedom."

"Hoots toots" curmurred the cushie doo. "Abeen aa, it maun soun weel."

"Na, na", skirled the ern. "The merk o a guid poem is the picturs it sets inby yer broo."

"Ye're wrang, aa o ee", argied the mavis. "Ye maun learn tae wauk afore ye can rin. Ye maun LEARN TAE THINK AFORE YE STERT TAE SCREIVE."

"CHI-CHI-chi-chi-chi-chi-cheee" cried the yalla yeitie. "Be quate, be quate, be quate, an haud yer wheeshts. Gin ye canna agree amangst hersels, the hoolet maun wyle a bard frae wir mids hissel."

The hoolet runkled his feathers and hodged frae fit tae fit, garrin them aa wyte fur his summation. Efter a lang cogitate, he gaed his repon. "Ae birdie's haen little tae say at this collogue," he said, "an yon's the magpie. Step forrit brither magpie. I wad hear fit *ye* think wad makk a guid bard fur the birdies."

"Losh, yon's a teuch nut tae crack richt eneuch", cawed the magpie. "Fur nane that's spukken the day hae telt a lee. A bard maun be skeely's a peinter at makkin picturs. He maun pattern an reel an rhyme an wyve wi wirdies like ony fiddler or wyver, be wyce an thochtful, blythe an licht betimes, like life itsel. He maun ken the wyes o men as weel as birdies, fur we aa share the warld thegither. He maun hae the hint o the warlock, the secund-sichted an the philosopher aboot him, an the soun o his wirds on the lug maun be like the music o the burn, wi a skirp o sunlicht ower it. I cudna begin tae chuse a bard frae ma fiers aroon. I·am nae wirthy."

Noo, the hoolit raxxed his hairt-shaped heid richt roon, wi his een takkin aathing in, like twa sherp preens. Thrice times three his een tuik in the warld, an syne he spak. "I chuse the magpie tae be the birdies' bard – fur he will wyle the best an bonniest frae aathing, as a true bard sud dae, baith braid in thocht an wing."

Sae yon concludit the Collogue o the birdies, an tae this verra day, Magnus the magpie is bard ower aa the winged fowk o the air. Bit takk tent, oh humankind, niver tae leave onythin braw or bonnie aboot his airt, or Magnus will nip it awa, tae wyve it inno his neist poem!

1, 2, 3: *Dali*, Dawn Ades, Thames & Hudson, 1982
4, 5, 6, 7: *Magritte*, Suzi Gablik, Thames & Hudson, 1984
8, 9, 10: *Zen in the Art of Helping*, David Brandon, Routledge, 1984
11, 12: *The Buddhist Way of Action*, Christopher Humphreys, Mandala Books, 1989
13: *Yoga & You*, James Hewitt, Tandem, 1974
14: *Yoga*, Ernest Wood, Penguin, 1969
15: *The Silent Teaching*, Sri Chinmoy, Citadel Books, 1985
16: *Letters to a Young Poet*, Rainer Maria Rilke,

Frank Kuppner

Scotland: A Winter's Tale

When the mighty Saint Columba
Wanted to set up an abbey
On the island of Iona,
He was greatly baulked by demons.

Loudly he implored the Lord to
Look with favour on his efforts
To install a modest chapel
By the margin of the breakers.

Every time that he attempted
Such a feat, the local spirits,
Angry at the rude intrusion,
Interfered and caused confusion.

Walls collapsing in the morning;
Walls collapsing in the evening;
Noonday meditations shattered
By the sound of walls collapsing.

Obviously, such a state of
Rank, unmitigated chaos
Simply could not be allowed to
Carry on ad infinitum.

Thus it was that Saint Columba,
Rudely wakened after midnight
In the middle of his prayers
By a dull, familiar rumbling

Which betokened the dispersal
Into rubble of the latest
Effort at cathedral-building,
Hurried tight-lipped from his cave-like

Cell, towards his neighbour's cloister –
Troubled as he did so by the
Even louder rumbling which he
Now could hear. Was all of Scotland

Toppling into desolation?
Poor, unhappy, Godless nation!
Only when he reached the doorway
Did he recognise the sound as

Merely the stupendous snoring
Of his friend the wise St. Oran.
Giving him a damn good shaking,
"Oran!" he called out, "Awaken!"

Oran (this means 'song' in Gaelic –
And the plural – 'songs' – is 'orain')
Knew at once from the expression
On Columba's face what ailed him.

"Gone again then, has it, guv'nor?"
He enquired. "Hell and Damnation!
Something must be done about it.
I've been giving it some thinking.

Look, Columba. It's them demons!
It's them demons; they're the culprits!
Something must be done about them!
Something must be done, I tell you."

"Yes, but what?" – replied Columba,
Secretly regretting that he
Hadn't simply stretched himself out
Horizontal on his mattress,

Rather than resorting to this
Superannuated so-called
Sage. "I know fine well it's demons.
What I want to know is how we

Manage to outsmart them, Oran.
What ideas on that one have you?"
Oran sighed. He gazed in silence
Upwards to the rough-hewn ceiling

Barely higher than their tonsures."
Then he cleared his throat and
Answered. "Lately I have been
Consulting various religious textbooks

A propos this very subject.
Things are not entirely hopeless.
Oh, it's difficult, I grant you,
But it's not entirely hopeless.

Theophrastodentolidos
(Blessed be his name for ever!)
Somewhere states – and his opinion
Counts for much among churchmen –

Macillmore of Troon, for instance,
Always bows to his opinion,
As does Bert in Castle Douglas.
Anyway, this Theophrasto –

Theophrastoden – this Theo-
Phrestodan – this Theophree – this
Theophrastodontolides
(Blessed be his name for ever!)

Gives a remedy for use in
Cases such as ours, where spirits
Seek to interfere, perhaps through
Moral or through legal scruples

With the bona fide building
Of religious edifices –" "What? What's
that?" exclaimed Columba:
"Are you seriously telling

Me that we can get our own back
On these irritating creatures?
Really? Truly? Oh, Cher Maître,
Put me out my misery at

Once. Oh, tell me! What's the answer?
Vengeance! Ah! Revenge! Vengeance!"
There was silence for a moment –
Save that breakers in the distance

Beat in sadness on the shore, and
One or two ejaculations
Floated on the balmy air from
Neighbouring recluses. Oran

Pursed his lips and answered: "It is
Fairly simple in a way. We
Need a member of our tribe, a
Fellow-monk; one who has never –

Not in any way whatever –
Had the very least scintilla,
Erm… of erm… of carnal knowledge
With a poor benighted sinner."

"What was that?" Columba asked him.
"It's the remedy for demons,"
Answered Oran. "All we need is
Someone who is wholly pure, who's

Willing to be buried in the
Precincts of the adumbrated
Sanctified construction. "Buried?"
Asked Columba. "To be buried?

Isn't that a little awkward?
There's the problem, to begin with,
That we're all alive." "The problem,"
Interposed the Blessed Oran,

"Is a little less straightforward.
Firstly, we must find this pure one
In our monkish ranks, and then we
Have to bury him alive." "What?"

Cried Columba. "But that's murder!
How on earth can anybody
Hope to sanctify a building
Through a murder? It's barbaric!

It's outrageous! What a monstrous
Proposition to advance to
Someone of my standing! Monstrous!
Let us hear no more about it!"

Softly, in the damp, ascetic
Cell, the endless condensation dripped
And dripped and dripped. The spider
Carried on with its remorseless

Occupation. Holy Father
Awkwardly, disconsolately
Looked at Holy Father. Oran
Cleared his throat, and tentatively

Made the following suggestion.
"Maybe I am missing something,
Sage and Master – but the setup –
Stop me if I'm wrong – is surely

Based on the devout assumption
Of the true believer, that the
Lord Creator of this goodly
Sphere, this earth, and all around it

Must be duty-bound to save his
Faithful servant from the threatened
Suffocation. What do you think?"
Saint Columba frowned. "Perhaps if

I could hear the text verbatim?"
"Certainly," replied his holy
Partner. "Let me read it to you.
'Forasmuch as the aforesaid –'"

"Wait a moment," interrupted
Saint Columba. "What I mean is:
There are only seven of us
On the island; and I want to

Find out which of us might still be
Eligible. Could you read me
Only sections appertaining
To the favoured definition

Here assigned to virtue. Must he
Be a virgin?" "Let me see," said
Oran testily, and scanned the
Sacred text. "Yes, yes. He must be.

Let me read the whole damn section.
'Also he must not have looked at
Any of his fellows bathing
With too keen an eye. Nor must he

Ever have frequented any
Overly convenient cupboard
Through the door of which, beause of
Flaws in the construction, he was

Able to observe the cooks, or
Serving-girls or other suchlike
Females doing what they did when
Solitary and relaxed. Nor

Must the chosen one have blundered
Into anybody's bedroom
Late at night, somnambulating
Uncontrollably, until the

Person forcibly removed him,
Using scissors, or perhaps a
Sleep-evaporating needle – '"
(Here Columba coughed, and turned a

Settled gaze towards the leafy carpet,
Feigning nonchalance which he was
Far from feeling). "Likewise, He must
not have slapped nor spanked nor

Leathered, thrashed, whacked,
flagellated, buffeted, belaboured,
pummelled, Birched, tanned, drubbed,
flogged, Trounced, whipped, larruped,
Scourged nor bastinadoed children's

Buttocks, more than absolutely
Necessary to correct their
Infelicities in grammar.
Finally, a word on donkeys – '"

"Stop!" Columba cried. "It's hopeless!
Hopeless! Hopeless. Why continue?
No-one, no-one in our outfit
Qualifies. We'll never build it."

"No-one?" Oran softly echoed.
"Haven't you forgotten something?
Haven't you forgotten something
Relevant? No? What's my nickname?"

"Oran the Aroma?" answered
Columb nervously, not seeing
How this helped. "No, not 'Aroma',"
Said the other sharply to his

Innocent detractor – "I have
Never heard that till this moment.
'Oran, Chaster than the Chastest',
That is what I meant. The Modest

Monk; Most Virtuous of Virgins;
Continent and Decent Oran.
Such am I reputed, such a
One am I indeed." "Good Heavens!"

Answered Columb. "We had always
Somehow thought your protestations
Must have been exaggerated."
"All were true," said Oran nobly.

"That you thought me such a liar,
Such a constant, unrepentant
Hypocrite, I must admit is something
Of a shock" "Good heavens!"

Said his mentor for the second
Time within as many minutes;
"Not at all! But such perfection
Seemed so outwith human frailty;

Seemed so far beyond the bounds of
Human possibility, that –
Oran: let me beg forgiveness."
Oran let him beg forgiveness.

In the morning, all assembled
Near the latest pile of rubble.
Disenchantment, melancholy,
Tiredness, sometimes even downright

Mutiny stood clearly figured,
Etched in each monastic visage.
We are saved, Columba told them.
We will build our chapel shortly,

Have no fear. And then he uttered
Fully, but perhaps without the
Wealth of circumstantial detail
Found above, the story of the

Night's events, and the ensuing
Revelations from Saint Oran.
What tumultuous applauding
Greeted the great man. He stepped out

Solemnly in front of them, and
Gave at once the necessary
Orders. Seized with joyous visions,
All began to dig with fervour.

Soon a pleasantly capacious
Excavation lay before them,
Into which the good Saint Oran
Briskly stepped. His grateful compeers

Thereupon began forthwith to
Fill the circumambient crater,
Till at length the good Saint Oran
Vanished utterly from sight as

Earth returned to its primeval
Haunts around his knees, his hips, his
Chest, his neck, his head, and so on.
Thus was Chastity's great martyr,

Still alive, ensevelated.
How his fellow-monks admired such
Stoicism, such forbearance
Under such extreme conditions.

"We could never have endured it,"
Whispered each one to his shovel-
Handling neighbour. As the barren
Earth began to pass the martyr's

Chin, it seemed to some onlookers,
More endowed with scruples than
Their Fellow-immolators, that the
Scapegoat might be undergoing

Something of a trauma. Something,
Even, like a late conversion
To the notion of survival.
Something not too unlike terror

Seemed to them to occupy his
Ever-moving eyes. Suggestions
Possibly connected with a
Change of heart about departure

Animated his beleaguered
Lips, as bits of terra firma
Started to descend his windpipe.
Nostrils first succumbed, then eyelids

Desperately beating, till at
Last the sole remainder was his
Noble tonsured dome, protruding
From his sudden mausoleum.

It was left to Saint Columba,
With his tried and tested shovel
To perform the stately topping-
Out upon the glowing bald patch.

"Rest there; rest there, faithful Oran,"
He intoned (redundantly, some
Thought), "secure in the safekeeping
Of the Lord, till we return for

You, when we have built our chapel
Here beside your humble gravestone."
Some were seen to weep; some
Shivered. All beside that grim location

Felt a certain perturbation.
"He will be alive," Columba
Reassured them, "when we dig up
His remains, on the completion

Of our Celtic Church. So, bearing
That in mind, it ill behoves us
Not to start immediately
Working on that job. The sooner

We can finish it, the sooner
We can disinter Saint Oran
Out from his unventilated chamber.
Friends, to work! To work, friends!"

Thus they set about constructing,
For the 17th or 18th
Time, their longed-for monastery:
Hammering and sawing, banging,

Raising, lowering, dismantling,
Re-erecting, bringing hither,
Taking thither, shouting orders,
Going off for meals, denying

Blame, disputing measurements and
Thicknesses – in fact, extremely
Similar to all that recent
Reconstruction work in Oran

Street, a thoroughfare not far from
Where I stay at present. It has
Changed completely. It has almost
Disappeared. A grass-lined pathway

Trickles past some fine new houses,
Leaving only a vestigial
Remnant of its former substance
At its southern end. The rest is,

Frankly, better gone. It was a
Fairly dreadful place. Depressing
Me each time I travelled through it –
Almost always on a bus. I

Do remember once, in childhood,
Being taken there by schoolfriends,
After school, to play. They lived there,
Not too far away from where they

Underwent their education.
And, with children being children,
Tea-time came, and they abandoned
Me upon the street, completely

Lost. In evergrowing panic,
Asking strangers for directions –
(None of whom had ever heard of
Either of the streets I wanted,

Fairly nearby though they were). I
Finally was taken in by
People living in a house which
Stood inside another schoolyard.

(Nowadays, I cross this schoolyard
When I go to vote. In those days,
Though I passed within a minute's
Walk of it five days a week, I

Might as well have been on Venus.)
I remember vaguely how a
Fire was burning, with a woman
Sitting near it, while the husband

Phoned my mother. Not long after,
They arrived (my parents) in that
Bafflingly real room. They thanked my
Kind protectors, and departed.

Strange, the bridges errant children
Build, constructed in a moment;
In a moment deconstructed.
This adventure has no sequel.

Anyway, the only reason
Why I mention this, is so that
Time enough can pass for Columb's
Men to get their chapel finished.

Now, at last, their work is finished.
Proudly, they stand back, admiring
Its robust, yet, somehow, graceful
Structure, one which has withstood the

Transatlantic gales which raged from
Time to time, and the nocturnal
Workings of whatever agents
Were abroad at nights. It stands there,

Proudly, whole and uncorrupted
By the elements, a tribute
Both to God, who has evoked its
Homage, and to him who made it

Possible, by sacrificing
Petty personal convenience
So that others, through his loss would
Gain infinities. They turn and

Look down at the rough, discoloured
Patch of earth, beneath which Oran
Either waits impatiently for
Their return, or decomposes.

Which is it to be, they wonder.
Slowly they approach the gravestone.
Ought they not perhaps to leave him?
Is it risking disappointment

Trying to recover from the
Bowels of the earth, a person
Buried there for 12 or 13 Weeks?
For, though they worked as quickly,

Putting up their kirk, as safety
Let them do – the fact remains that
No-one, under the conditions
Oran was preserved in, ought to

Last for weeks. Such doleful thoughts
Were present in all minds. But
Columb, seemingly interpreting the
Silence common to them all as

Reticence, exhorted them as
Follows. "Fellow friars, friends and
Acolytes – here lies a hero.
Altruistically aiming

Outwards, seeking the salvation
Only of outsiders, Oran
Gave his life, or the appearance
Of his life, that we might finish

Off this self-appointed task. He
Lies here, just below this surface,
Waiting for his friends, his colleagues,
Trusted quite without compunction,

Trusted with his life, to honour
Their agreement, and to rescue
Him from his untimely, cruel
Tomb. How can we even think of

Leaving him to rot forever
In those Stygian depths from which no
Traveller – er, that's to say in
Which no-one could fail to hail the

Prospect of release. So, brothers:
Underneath that heap of pebbles
Lies our saviour (in the lesser sense, Of
course). He, thanks to whom, we

Now possess that splendid chapel
At our backs." (Here he, assaulted
By a sudden doubt, looked round. But
Yes, the glorious erection

Still was standing where he'd left it.)
"Friends, I say to you, pick up your
Shovels; grasp your spades; and join
me. Now or never is the moment

Ripe for digging up the carcass
Of a buried celibate and
Martyr. Will you join me, brothers?"
In response, he heard a chorus,

Deafening the timid breakers
With their cries of, "Cursed be he who
Fails to help in our attempt to
Disinter the sacred body

Lying underneath our sandals!"
What a sight it was that followed
Their concerted exclamations.
Incoherently, they started

Scrabbling at the vulnerable
Surface of the grave. Columba,
Fearful what this dangerously
Hectic, uncoordinated

Energy might have upon the
Relics, instantly commanded
Care and tact. This was complied with.
Delicately they removed the

Topmost layer, and unearthed the
Wizened, balding surface of the
Subterranean saintly skull. The
Next manoeuvre called for all the

Careful handiwork for which the
Celt is justly celebrated. Delicately,
The detritus, coarse-engrained by
now, was swept off

Oran's reappearing head. To
Gasps of wonder – for it seemed that
All was as before, except that
None discerned the slightest sign of

Life. Some whispered:" Is he
Breathing?" Gingerly, the excavation
Carried onwards to the thorax.
Still no signs of life. Then down to

Oran's hips and paunch, which
seemed as comfortably well-
upholstered as before. But still there
was no clear, conclusive indication

Showing life to have continued.
Not until his knees were almost
Clear of earth, did he begin to
Tremble slightly. What a ripple

Coursed through the august assembly.
"Look!" "Look there!" "Look there – he
trembles!" Feverishly they released him
Almost to the very ankles,

Wildly, indiscriminately
Throwing mud and dirt away from
Oran's now spasmodically
Heaving body. Then, as if a

Pure, unprecedented surge of
Pressure had been detonated
Deep within him, he emerged from
Out his dwam, and, with impatience,

Plucked his feet from their
emplacements, leaving in their stead a
muddy pair of prints. At once, he
scrambled upwards, from his informal

Sepulchre. A fit of coughing
Overtook him, as he tried to
Clear his throat of the obstructions
Stopping him from speaking. Columb

Stretched his loving arms towards him.
"Hail! Our Saviour! Thou whose choice
to suffer in our stead has freed us
From the clutches of those demons,

Whose perversity prevented
Us from hitherto completing
Our divine appointed mission!"
Here he paused, and Oran struggled

To reply, but, still unused to
Worlds where speech was possible, he
Signalled to him to continue.
"There behind us," he proceeded,

"Stands the building which you
bravely, nay, which you heroically
Skirted death for. If you like, we
Might proceed there, haec instante.

We could offer up some prayers;
Hymns of gratitude for such a
Magical, or let us rather
Call it, so miraculous a

Safe deliverance as this your
Marvellous return to us from
Underneath the earth, despite the
Length of your incarceration

Under such malign conditions.
You will get your voice back there, I
Rather fancy. To the chapel!"
"No, no, no, no, no, no – never!"

Cried Saint Oran, after one last
Monumental struggle with his
Shattered vocal system. "Never!"
Let us pause here for a moment,

To consider this amazing scene.
A man returning from a lengthy
Passage of existence, mole-like,
Underneath the tight-packed

Surface of the earth, on one side.
On the other side, a group of
Founders of a new religion –
All regarding the returning

Figure, clearly unsure whether
Human being, wraith, or spectre
Standing before them. Still the breakers
throw themselves upon Iona –

Punctuations in the silence
Lengthening between the parties
On the shore. Quite obviously,
Anyone who has been buried

As a favour to oneself, who
Posthumously re-emerges
(Talking hypothetically
For the moment – Oran's status

Still is far from clear to those who
Hear his outburst) must be listened
To attentively. The basic
Logic of the situation

Clearly calls for this. More breakers
Hit the shoreline; more and more the
Sense of magic previously
Felt begins to dissipate as

Nothing happens to resolve the
Tension. "Did I understand you,
Brother Oran?" asked Columba.
"Did you not express reluctance

When the possibility of
Coming with us to the chapel,
Newly built, our own the labour
Which completed it – or have I

Somehow failed to grasp your
Meaning?" Certainly you grasped my
Meaning," answered Oran with a
Shudder. I have not the least intention

Now or ever in the furthest
Future of repairing to the
Sanctum of your superstition,"
(Gasps were heard), "alone, or in a

Band of equally deluded
Crazed, idolatrous neurotics."
"Oran! Oran!" cried Columba.
"This is not the same old Oran!

This is not the man who gladly
Sung the praises of the Godhead
Hours on end. Something has
Happened." "Certainly it has," said Oran.

"I at least derived some profit
In my underground seclusion.
Things became extremely clear to
Me – beginning from the moment

When the earth rose up above my
Eyelids." "He's become a Muslim!"
Someone whispered in the monkly
Entourage – a brilliant feat of

(Quite unsound) prognostication,
Given that divine Mahomet
Hadn't yet been born. "Become a
What?" his scorn-filled voice demanded.

"All of this religious business –
Take my word for it – is nonsense.
There is not a word of truth in
Any of this talk of Gods and

Spirits. Not a word. Admit it!"
Gasps were heard from the
Surrounding semicircle of his compeers.
Hurried prayers. Cries of anguish.

Imprecations such as, "Turncoat!
Heretic! Blasphemer! Pagan!
Infidel!" But he continued
Calmly on his way. "I tell you –

I have died and you have not died.
I have seen what's to be seen, and,
More important, what is never
Seen, in any circumstances.

There is no creator. Nothing.
No Last Judgement. Not a trace of
Anything like Hell or Heaven –
Nothing. Waken up! The sheerest

Lies and fantasies sustain you.
Cast those falsehoods off! Accept the
Truth of things while still you can, and
Turn towards the light. I've seen it!"

This tirade was met with ever-
Growing murmurs, culminating
Sharply in the throwing of a
Hail of stones towards the rebel.

"Stop!" cried Saint Columba. "Stop this!
It is not for us, my children,
To be judges of this sorry
Fall from grace. For who are we to

Know how such a devastating
Trial, such as our companion
Lately went.through, might not alter
Even our most firm convictions?

Let us try to understand his
Problems in the Christian spirit,
Such as was enjoined upon us
By our God." Shamefacedly, the

Gathered mystics saw the wisdom
Pregnant in the course of action
Adumbrated by Columba.
They disposed themselves to listen,

Ready to extend forgiveness,
Should they have to – and Columba
Turned, his noble face the very
Model of compassion, to his

Weak, disorientated colleague.
"Oran! Friend! Reflect! Consider!
You have undergone a hellish
Trial. But what power, think you,

Was it, which has brought you back to
These your friends? Your very
Presence testifies to the Almighty's
Potency. Without the Godhead

Guarding you, how could you be here?
You have been through an ordeal which
ought by rights to have extinguished
Each last spark of life. How comes it

You have triumphed over such as
Suffocation, cold, exposure,
Damp, starvation, lack of drinking
Water; and returned to tell the

Tale – though not, alas, the tale which
Ought by rights to have been told us?
Think! How is it possible that
Someone could endure such hardship,

Were there not a God above us,
Giving personal assistance
In our hour of need? Your silence
Adequately gives the only

Feasible response. Come, Oran!
Come! Our new-built church awaits us."
Angrily, the shade (if such he
Was) rebuffed the offered hand of

Friendship. "Ask me not the whys and
"Wherefores," he exclaimed: "the fact is,
I was there, and I saw nothing
Even vaguely corresponding

To the nonsense which our dogmas
Tell us is the truth. It's rubbish!
Drivel! Sheer infatuation!
Nothing like it ever has or

Ever will exist, I tell you!
God does not exist, despite the
Casuistical farrago
You have lately offered. Heaven

Is on earth or nowhere – likewise
Hell." (The first stone hit him.)
"Likewise useless is the old Distinction
into soul and body. After

Death we vanish, as before it
We did not exist – not as a
Soul or star or fish or flower,
Stone, or vague emotive power,

Drifting idly through the cosmic
Space." (A second pebble hit him.)
"Things emerge, things disappear, and
Local pools of interaction

Throw up objects such as us, or
Such as those small rocks which now
You hurl towards me. In the end, it
Comes to much the same." A well-aimed

Rock here hit him on the forehead,
Causing him to stagger back and
Fall into the pit from which he
Lately had emerged. Columba

Watched him, with increasing sadness,
Disappear beneath the growing
Heaps of stones and dirt a second
Time. At last his flushed disciples

Called a halt to their exertions.
Once again an eerie silence
Settled onto fair Iona;
Onto monks surrounding with a

Curiously shame-faced air the
Heap of pebbles underneath which
Lay the dead or not dead Oran.
Breakers fell upon the shoreline;

Curlews looped the skies. A last few
Stones, no longer necessary,
Fell unwanted on the cooling earth.
"Look there. The sun has almost

Set," Columba said, and gestured
Vaguely at the sea. "The evening
Took us in its grasp before we
Even noticed. Now our solemn

Task has been completed, and the
Building stands before us, waiting
Patiently for our arrival.
What could be a more auspicious

Time for an inaugurating
Ceremony? Let us form a
Chaste procession, fitting for a
Formal entrance to a building

Which, at times, I'm sure we never
Thought to live to see. Yet there it
Stands. Come, brethren, it awaits us."
Off they moved towards their chapel,

Solemn, stately, noble; thinking
Holy thoughts appropriate to
Such a moment. Disappearing
Piously beneath its lintels

One by one – the final entrant
Pulling shut the door, which caused the
Building to collapse in ruins,
Trapping all of them inside it.

Maureen Macnaughtan

New Town

You can sense the sound of traffic
across parks as big as Alaska.
Here the air is glacier fresh
in the distance endless valleys.
Birds are always flying through paradise.

Let Dorset claim the plough boy
and a landscape scorched in tradition,
we are too insistent for vine Gods.
Ariel magic and ice-cream bells
provide an indispensable religion.

Postcards belong to hot summer places
where the boats are for rent.
Before leaving experience the bowling alley
the pins are a wild extravagance
they blaze on Saturday nights.

In this concrete studio with gorse
plastic tulips hug the horizon.
The hills are duly rabbited,
fern sculpture adds to the solace
of a personal nest in stone.

Can you hear them chanting
"Have I won a way out?"

Goths

Huddled around the civilizing neon
The lure of religion
Feeds the still-lifes.
There are bulls among the coven
Heavy with chains and skulls,
They worship without a temple
Recognising the need to be.

In mourning for the universe
A generation of tailored black
Condemn the material world.
Viewed as one great mass,
Reeling from the mess we've created
Exposure keeps these Grimm fairy-tales
Superior in their serenity.

The martyrs live to finger-paint,
To hurt by deforming beauty
As part of the tribal ordeal.
Each figure is a demonstration:
Red twists on dramatic mouths
Link this lean, green bloodstock.
Another decade and the great reviver
Unwinds the old cult-clock.

Armchair Ghosts

The sick squat in the dust,
Some are so ashamed
They hide their rag bones
Until the lens moves on.
The flames that were warm
Now welcome the condemned,
Infants with old men's eyes
Hang on withered breasts.

The camera angle widens
Following the river course
The dry, dirt-bed of nothing.
The barefoot line disappears
Along with another chocolate.
I gaze at the pot-plants
Standing in their own well.
Eager paws attack the door.

We retreat to the garden
And the dying are persistent,
They will not go away.
Frail, agonized ghosts
Circle on the bird table
Demanding a crumb of life.
Our world is freezer full
A feast of rigor mortis.

Illustration by Keith Clark

Tom Flannigan & Rob Griffith

Quendale Bay

A New Year dawning, fair and free
This January, ninety three
The seas are high, the skies are grey
Disaster's but a wave away.

> Quendale, Quendale, wind and rain
> When will your seas be clean again?

Black as night, the rich man's gold
Spilling from the stricken hold
With broken back the Braer lay
And poured destruction on that day.*(Chorus)*

Man's endless greed for easy gain
Assails the land with an oily rain
And children's lungs the price must pay
Of a tanker's death in Quendale bay.*(Chorus)*

Seals and seabirds choked and oiled
A century of nature spoiled
The sanctuary opened wide
Our future ebbing with the tide.*(Chorus)*

The Cave of Gold

Lorn Macintyre

"Try the first verse again," her mother said.

Catriona stood, composing herself, her hands together.

Is truagh mi rìgh gun tri làmhan,
Da làimh 'sa phìob, da làimh 'sa phìob...

My sorrow that I don't have three hands,
Two for the pipes, two for the pipes,
My sorrow that I don't have three hands,
Two for the pipes, one for the sword.

Her father was sitting with a leg over the arm of his chair, watching her. She kept her eyes on his dangling cigarette as she sang.

"That was much better, wasn't it, Archie?" her mother said. "You're going to win it, my pet." She was nine years old and was entering the medal competition in the island Mod with 'Uamh an Oir', 'The Cave of Gold'. Her mother used to hum the tune to her as she was putting her to bed.

"I learnt it from my mother. It's about a piper who gets a silver chanter from a beautiful girl who plays the harp. I'll teach you the song one day."

Catriona liked to fall asleep listening to her mother humming the song. She dreamt of a cave with a dazzling opening in the darkness. Inside was a bicycle made of gold, with a little pouch hanging from the saddle. Her mother had been a good singer, and they said that she'd inherited her voice. But she'd never heard her father sing. He came from an island further north, and his Gaelic had strange hard words. Some nights she heard her parents quarrelling in the bedroom, and once something hit the wall.

The croft was isolated and she had to play by herself, going up and down the rough road with her doll in the pram. On the nights when her mother was out at the Rural or visiting relatives her father put her to bed. She told him she could undress herself, but he liked to help. One night he'd touched her. She thought it was an accident, but he did it again.

"I know what you would like," he said.

She didn't say anything.

"And I'm going to get it for you. It's a secret. Don't tell Mammy."

He touched her the next night her mother went to the Rural then helped her to dress again and took her by the hand out to the shed in the darkness. She was frightened, but he snapped on the light. A red fairy cycle was leaning against his workbench. Her mother had been promising her one for the last few Christmases. She'd never seen anything so beautiful. The handlebars gleamed, and the spokes threw shadows on the shed floor. There was a label tied to the saddle, with her name and three crosses for kisses. He sat her on it in her nightdress and wheeled her about under the stars in the warm night. She wanted him to carry it up the stairs to her bedroom.

"Mammy will make a row. I'll leave it in the porch, it'll be safe there."

Mairi almost fell over the bicycle when she came back from the Rural with the baking she'd won the prize for. "That's spoiling her, Archie. It could have waited for her birthday. Or you could have got her a second-hand one. There are adverts in the paper. Kids grow out of them."

"I sold the calf for a good price," he said, shrugging his shoulders.

The bicycle had a bell and a basket on the front. He went up and down the road with her, holding on to the back of the saddle and the handlebars until she could keep her balance. The lapwings were tumbling from the sky as she rode up and down, ringing the bell for the pleasure of hearing the sound while he ploughed the field on the old smoky Fordson. She leaned her bicycle carefully against the grassy verge so that she wouldn't chip the red paint, and laid the flowers she picked into the basket on the handlebars for her mother, who'd started to teach her 'The Cave of Gold'.

Ead'rainn a' chruit, a' chruit, a' chruit...

Between us the harp, the harp, the harp,
Between us the harp, my friends and I parted,
Between us her song, her song, her song...

Her father clapped, the cigarette in his mouth.

"Why are you standing like that?" her mother asked.

"I'm sore," she said, looking at her father.

"Sore? Where?"

"You're embarrassing her, Mairi," he said. "It'll be the saddle; I'll adjust it."

She stood looking at her feet, couldn't get the words out. She knew it was hopeless, her mother would never believe her. In the pain of her silence she saw his cigarette ash fall to the carpet. He scuffed it with his shoe.

"Off you go to bed now," her mother said.

"I've got homework to do," Catriona said, going for her bag.

"But you don't get homework in primary," her mother said. "Why are you getting so difficult about going to bed? All this excitement about learning a song? How are you going to be when you're on the platform?"

"She'll be just fine," her father said.

"I'll make you Horlicks so that you'll sleep," her mother said.

She held the mug with the frothy white liquid in both hands, taking as long as possible to drink it. Her father was watching her, smiling.

"Time for bed," her mother said, taking the mug from her. "Daddy will come in and tuck you up."

Though it was summer the bedroom was cold. She stood at the window in the coomed wall, looking across the machair to the mountains over the Sound, wishing she was a bird. She would go there and never come back, make a nest in a high cliff where nothing could reach her. She was shaking as she took off her clothes. She pulled on the nightdress with the red bow at the neck, then slipped into the bed, making herself into a tight ball under the duvet. She heard his footstep on the stair. The door opened and closed, the bed moving as he sat down. Then he stretched out beside her.

"You sing that song really well. You're going to get the medal, you know."

She didn't answer.

When he put his hands under the clothes she thought of the Cave of Gold. As she learnt more of the song it was becoming a frightening place. The piper had been given a silver chanter so that he could play better than anyone, but after a year and a day he had to go down into the dark cave.

"Our secret," he said, smoothing back her hair. "It's our secret. Ay, you're going to get the medal and I'm going to buy you a big bicycle with special things on it. That's our secret." He said she could ride it to school, and he would get lights fitted for the dark nights. The next day she had a puncture on the road, a bent nail from a horseshoe. She was in tears as she looked at the deflated tyre, as if the bicycle was ruined. But he was coming over the field, holding down the barbed wire as he crossed the fence.

"We'll sort it," he said, squatting on his heels beside her and putting his arm round her shoulders. "Away to the shed for my tool box."

He removed the wheel and levered off the tyre, smeared adhesive on the gash in the tube, put a patch on it and rubbed the repair with blue chalk.

"We'll let it dry for a few minutes," he said before he screwed on the pump. "Here, you do it." He gripped the tyre as it got harder. "There you are now, good as new. There aren't many things that can't be sorted."

They had spoken Gaelic to her even before they spoke English to her. She was the best in her class and knew more words than anyone else. They wanted her to be a teacher, but she didn't like Gaelic now.

He went away, and she lay sobbing. She was frightened to go to sleep because she knew she would have a nightmare about the Cave of Gold. Her mother told her the story that wasn't in the song. The piper's dog had come running out of it mad-eyed and hairless, but there was no sign of the piper. An old woman at a well some distance from the cave could hear the sound of his pipes beneath her feet, a wail of despair from the darkness.

"What's happening to you, Catriona?" the teacher asked when she gave back the Gaelic test. "You used to be top of the class, but now you're making silly mistakes. It's weeks since you got a gold star. And stop fidgeting in your seat as if you've got ants in your pants." The other children laughed.

"We'll try that verse again," her mother said after tea.

He was sitting watching her.

"I can't remember," Catriona said.

"*Can't* remember! Went over it three times last night?" her mother said, irritated. "You're not paying attention. You're spending too much time on that bike. I'll tell you the words once and then you sing them."

> Bidh na minn bheaga nan gobhair chreagach,
> Mun tig mise, mun till mise a Uamh an Oir...
>
> *The little kids will be goats of the crags*
> *Before I arrive, before I return from the Cave of Gold...*

"I'm going away to aunt Jessie's for the weekend. You can sing to Daddy."

She wanted to run after the car as her mother drove away, to tell her everything, but somehow she couldn't. She lay listening to the sound of the television set below, putting her fingers down her throat, trying to be sick. He came up as the cliffs across the Sound were darkening.

"I'll just lie here till you go to sleep."

She didn't want to fall asleep in case he touched her. But then he went away and she closed her eyes. She was in the Cave of Gold, with arms around her in the darkness. Now a goat was pushing against her. When she woke she felt the pain inside her and beat him away with her fists.

"I'll tell Mammy what you did!" When she saw the blood on the sheet she began to moan in terror.

"No, no," he said, rocking her in his arms. "It'll be all right."

She found it difficult going down the stairs next morning because of the pain. He wasn't there. She didn't make herself any food because she was feeling sick. She sat staring at the wall until she heard his pick-up. The door opened and he wheeled in a red bicycle with gold bands. She sat looking at it. It had handlebars that swept down, and many gears, and a dynamo.

"Try it," he said. He wheeled it outside and held it for her while she put her feet into the straps on the pedals. But it was painful, sitting in the saddle. She rode it down the track, standing up on the pedals. She looked back and saw him watching her at the gable of the croft. It was fifteen miles to her auntie's, where Mammy was staying, but he would catch up with her in the pick-up and no one would believe her, because he'd taken the sheet off the bed and put it into the washing machine.

If she took the bicycle he would keep on touching her. But it was beautiful and as she rode up the track to the house she moved the lever and felt the chain slackening and tightening again as the gears shifted. When she was about fifty yards from where he was waiting she twisted the handlebars violently and lay on the ground moaning by the spinning wheel as he came running, tossing away his cigarette.

"I hit a stone. It's my leg."

He carried her upstairs, but when he tried to undress her she pretended to scream with the pain. "I think you should get the doctor," she sobbed.

"It'll be all right," he said. "You've twisted your leg. I'll take the wheel into town to get it straightened." He left her lying with her clothes on.

Mairi saw the new bicycle propped up against the wall when she drove up. She left the car door open and went to find him. He was at his workbench, filing something at the vice.

"This is the limit, Archie. Where did you get the money when I can't even get things for the house? The washing machine leaks every time I use it."

"She deserves it, for the effort she's put into the song," he said.

"Wouldn't it have been better waiting to see if she won the medal before getting that for her? You're spoiling her, Archie. When she goes to the big school she'll come to expect things. She'll never be off your back."

"It's a few years yet before she goes away. Besides, she's not that type of girl," he said, the file rasping.

"I wish we'd had a son instead, because you wouldn't have spoilt him like this," Mairi said heatedly. "You'll change her and you'll regret it."

Catriona heard the argument as she came round the corner.

"You're limping," her mother said accusingly.

"I fell off the bike."

"You could have broken your leg, after all that practice for the Mod. I hope you've been singing to Daddy while I was away."

The night before the Mod they went over the song for the last time.

"Don't stand with your fingers locked like that; it's a sign that you're nervous, and the judges will notice," her mother checked her.

Catriona took a breath as she'd been taught. Her mouth was open, but no words came.

"What's the matter?" her mother asked sharply.

"I can't remember."

"Can't remember? We've gone over the song a dozen times, and you a native speaker. If this happens tomorrow who's going to help you?

She ran from the room. She went round the gable of the house by the peat stack. The cliffs across the Sound were getting dark. The birds would be settled for the night on their ledges where nothing could reach them. But she had no safe place to go to. She was losing everything, even the language she'd been born with, the language her mother had sung her to sleep with, and there was no one to tell, not even in English.

She turned and saw the glow of his cigarette.

"You come back in and show Mammy you can do it," he said, taking her hand. "She wants you to get that medal and I'll buy you a gold chain for it."

Next morning she locked the door before having a bath, and put a chair against the door handle as she buttoned the new white blouse with frills her mother bought her. She zipped up the skirt in her father's dark tartan.

The hall was full for the competition. She was the last of the six to sing.

Is truagh mi rìgh gun trì lamhan...
My sorrow that I don't have three hands,
Two for the pipes, two for the pipes,
My sorrow that I don't have three hands,
Two for the pipes, one for the sword.

The judges were sitting forward in their chairs. They had put their marking pencils down and were listening. They had never heard the song performed with such emotion, and by someone so young. It was as if the girl on the platform was struggling in the darkness.

Bidh na laoidh bheaga nan cro-eadraidh
Mu tig mise, mun till mise a Uam an Oir...

The little calves will be milking cows
Before I arrive, before I return from the Cave of Gold...

Her parents were sitting in the front row. Her mother was wearing the medal she'd won for the same song. But Catriona was looking at her father. He wasn't smiling any more.

Siomadh maighdean òg fo cheud bhàrr
Theid a null, a theid a null...
Many a young untouched maiden
Will cross over, will cross over,
Before I return from the Cave of Gold.

Suddenly she felt the tightness around her slackening. She was emerging into the light as she sang the chorus for the last time.

Ead'rainn a luaidh, a luaidh, a luaidh...
Between us her song, her song, her song...

Her mother was on her feet, her arms out, but he was sitting with his face in his hands, his shoulders shaking.

Salvatore Quasimodo

Owerset by Alastair Mackie

Giorno Dopo Giorno
Day Aifter Day (1943–1946)

On the Sauch Boughs

And whit wey could we mak poems
wi the fremmit jackboot on oor hert,
amang the leavins o the deid i the squares
on the gress dour wi ice,
to the lamb-baein o the bairns,
the black skelloch o the mither meetin her son
crucifeet on the telegraph pole?
On the sauch boughs for an offrin
oor lyres were hung forby
sweein licht in the waesome wind.

Scrieve

This deid-dour silence in the streets,
this dwaumy wind that slips nou
laich through the deid leaves or lifts again
to the colours o the fremmit flags...
mebbe the sair need to say jist ae word
afore the lyft aince mair mirkens
ower anither day, mebbe sweerness,
oor meanest faut... This
isna life, this fearsome dark dirlin
o the hert, this peety,
it's nocht but a game the blood plays
when death's in flooer. O my douce gazelle
I mind that geranium o yours
bleezin on the bullet-howkit wa!
Och, does death nae mair console the livin,
nae even the death through love?

19 January 1944

I read ye liltin verses o antiquity,
words born o the vine-yairds and the tents
on the river-sides o the east,
hou doolful and dreich they drap doun nou
into this mirkest nicht o war

whaur naebody reenges the lyft
o the angels o death,
and ye hear the wind rummlin wi ruin
gin it blatter the sheet airn that up here
pairts the open balconies,
and the dirge o the dogs lifts yowlin
fae the gairdens at the rattle-shots o the guairds
in the toom streets. Somebody's alive.
Somebody's alive; mebbe. But us here,
spell-boond afore this auld-warld tongue,
we sik a sign that gaes ayont the dool o life,
the uncanny glamourie o the yirth,
whaur even amang ruckles o stane
the evil gress heists its ain flooer.

Snaw

Nicht faas; aince mair ye leave us
weel-looed images o the earth,
trees, beasts, poor fowk happit up
in sodgers' muckle coats, mithers
wi their wymes wizzent wi greetin.
And the snaw in the parks leams on us
like the moon. O thae deid fowk! Dirl
on your brou, dirl doun to the very hert.
Somebody skirl oot at least in the silence
in this snaw-white ring o the deid.

Day After Day

Day aifter day; damnèd words and the blood
and gowd. I ken ye, my peers, monsters o the yirth.
Peety has gaen doun afore your teeth,
and the blissit cross has left us.
Nae mair can I win back to my Elysium.
We'll bigg tombs on the sea strand, the huggert fields,
but nae monuments shall mark the heroes.
Mony's the time death has joukit us;
the air soughed wi a monotonous reeshle o leaves
like the watter-craw in the heather
that mounts a clood when the sirocco blaws.

Mebbe the Hert

It will sink doun, the keen tang o the lime-trees
intill this nicht o weet. The time o joy,
its teeth-brakkin levin-fire,

its rantin wudness, will be in vain,
The wey oot through sweernes is aa but shut,
the mindin o a gesture, a syllable,
but as a slow flaffin o birds through fog-reek.
And again, my tint ane, ye wait on for –
I dinna ken whit; mebbe the doom-hour
that reminds ye o the beginnin or the end,
the same weird by nou. Here the black smoor
fae the fires aince mair parches the thrapple.
Gin ye can, forget yon waff o brimstane
and the dreid. The words fair fash us,
they waal up fae staney watters;
mebbe the hert still bides wi us
mebbe the hert...

Winter Nicht

And aince mair the winter nicht,
and the dark splyters on the burgh tooer,
and the fogs that fooner the river
and the thorn-busses and bracken. O frien
ye hae tint your hert; the braid strath
hasna room eneugh for us.
Here in silence ye murn your land
and bite on your coloured hankie
wi a wolf's teeth;
dinna wauken the loon that asleeps aside ye
his nakit feet happit up in a hole.
Let naebody mind us o oor mithers, naebody
tell us a dream o hame.

Milan, August 1943

In vain ye socht amang the stour
poor hand; the city is deid.
It's deid; the last dunderin is heard
in the hert o the Naviglio. And the rossignol
has drappit fae the aerial, heich abune the convent,
whaur aince she sang afore the doon-sinking.
Dinna howk for waals in the court-yairds,
the livin are nae drouthy ony mair.
Dinna touch the deid, sae reid, sae swaalt;
leave them in the mools o their hooses;
the city is deid. Deid.

Heich Wa

And even nou on the heich wa o the stadium
through the bore-holes and tussocks o hinging gress
the lizards skimmer like lichtnin;
and the puddock cams back to the dyke-side,
the plain-sang o my nichts
in country-sides hyne awa. Ye mind this place
whaur the big starn hailed oor gloamin-tryst.
O love, hou muckle time has passit
wi the poplar leaves, hou muckle the bleed skailt
in the rivers o the earth!

O My Douce Beasts

Nou Aatumn blads the green o the hills,
o my douce beasts. Aince mair we'll hear
afore the mirknin, the last wheeple
o the birds, the bird – pleep o the grey carse
that meets the deep jumm o the sea.
And the smell o wud in the rain,
the reek o dens, hou keen here amang hooses
and in men, o my douce beasts.
This face whaur slow een swivel,
this hand that merks the lyft
whaur thunder reels are yours,
my wolves, my foxes, brennt wi bleed.
Ilkie hand and face are yours.
Ye tell me that aathing has been for nocht,
life – jist days nyauvit by the teeth o watter,
and a bairn-sang rises fae the gairdens.
Hyne awa fae us nou, is it?
But it mells wi the air like a shadow nearhand.
Yon is your voice.
But mebbe I ken
that aathing has nae been in vain.

Scrievit Mebbe on a Tomb

Here, hyne awa fae aathin the sun yarks
your hair and its hinny bleezes,
already fae the buss simmer's last cicala,
and the howe yowlin o the siren warnin
on the plains o Lambardy minds us
we are alive. O air-birstled voices
whit's your wull? Aince mair
languor rises fae the yirth.

Me a Pilgrim

Here's me back again in the quait square;
the streamer on your balcony wags its lane
for the gaudie-day already spent.
– show yoursel aince mair – I cry. But only
the age that hankers for the cheatry o enchantments
swickit the echo fae the howe-holes
o toom rock. O hou lang it's been since the unseen
gied nae answer when I cryit,
as aince I did, in the silence! Ye're here nae mair,
nae mair your words o welcome traivel to me,
a pilgrim nou. Still, joy unhaps
twa faces. The ootmaist licht
dings on the pine that minds on the sea.
And vain forby the image o the watters.

Oor land is hyne awa, in the Sooth
o het tears and murnin. Doon there
black-shawled weemin collogue aboot death
on the door-sills o their hooses.

Fae the Castle Craig o Heich Bergamo

Ye hae heard the cock's skraich in the air
ootowre the ramparts, beyond the tooers
gealin wi a licht ye didna ken o;
a fire-flaucht skelloch o life, and the reeshle
o voices ben in the cells, and the bird-ca
o the sentries afore the day-daw whitens.
And ye hadna a word for yoursel;
fae nou on ye were in a circle o sun-glaffs;
and the antelope and heron haed wheesht,
tint in a whuff o unchancy fog,
handsels o a warld as yet unborn.
And the Februar moon passit clear ower the yirth,
a lowe in its ain silence, but for you
it was only a ghaist in the mind.
You tae amang the cypress trees o the castle craig
pass on withoot a soond; and here anger
is stilled by the green o deid loons
and peety, hyne awa nou, is nearhand joy.

Near the Adda

The Adda craals by your side at mid-noon
and ye follow the whummelt shadda o the lyft.
Here, whaur sheep, boued neck-deep in the gress
rax up again, the watter loupit
to the shear o the wheel, and the grunstane
o the ile-press craikit and the olives
plunkit doun into the vat.
You alane fash yoursel in a vain feeroch.
The bourtree's croun keeks up again
fae the hert o the hedge and the rashes reeshle
new leaves on the river dykes. The life
that begunkt ye is in yon green flags,
the human yirth's salute
to the pu o stresses and the skailt bleed.
When the tree flushes aa ae green again
this is your certainty, like the swick
in your bleed, like the sweep o the hand
to the broo, a bield against the licht.

Again I Hear the Sea

For mony nichts nou I've heard the sea aince mair,
its sclimmin thunders, its soughin faals,
licht alang the sleek sands. Echo o a voice
lockit in the mind, risin up fae time; and
forby, this uncessant pleepin o the gulls;
mebbe o tooer birds that April airts forrit
to the plains. Aince ye were near me,
a neebor to yon voice, and I wish nou
it micht rise to you forby, this ech-
o memory o me, jist like
yon mirksome murmellin o the sea.

Elegy

Cauld avant-currier o the nicht
ye cam back again clear to the balconies
o ruined hooses to lichten
the unkent tombs, the toom lerrochs
o the reekin yirth. Here
sleeps oor dream. And aa your lane ye turn back
to the north whaur aathing hists to the deid
bar you. You haud on in the dark.

O Anither Lazarus

Fae the maist hyne back winters, thunder dings
a brimstane gong ower the reekin glens.
And as in yon time
the voice o the forest soughs; *Ante lucem*
a somno raputs, ex herba inter homines,
surges. And your stane whaur the image o the warld
swithers, is whummelt doun.

The Ferry

Whaur d'ye cry fae? Your voice is a hairse dirl
in the fog. Aince mair fae the bothies,
it is time, the hungry dogs breenge oot
for the river alang the scentit fit-paths;
skinklin wi bleed, the whittret snickers
to the ither bank. It's a ferry I ken;
black stanners bile up on the watter there,
and mony's the boat that passes in the nicht
wi their brunstane torches. Nou ye're already
hyne awa for sure, gin your voice gangs
stoondin on in undeemous echoins
and I can scarce hear its soughin faa.
But I see ye: ye hae violets in your fauldit hands,
sae ghaist-white, and lichens at your een.
And syne ye deid.

Your Silent Fit

And here's the sea and the agave in flooer already
and the colour o the river skinklin bricht
by auld-warld tombs josslin like bee-skeps
by the heich wa, and in keekin-glesses,
quines still lauchin, their black hair lowse.
And o them was aside ye
on the river banks o Ionia
– a bee lowed in her hinny-sleek ee –
and left scarce the licht o a name
in the olives' shaddaw. Naebody to save ye nou;
ye ken that ae day daws on your face
the same's the lave; a quick cheengin o licht
roond the ring that locks us in ticht,
ayont the howe-hole o the moon
whaur your silent fit crosses ower Hades.

Man O My Time

Ye're still yon-ane-wi-the-stane-and-the-sling,
man o my time. Ye were there in the cockpit
wi the deevil's wings, the sun-dials o death,
– I've seen ye – inside the chariots o flame, at the dool-tree,
at the cairt wheels o torture. Aye, I've seen ye,
it was you, wi your exact science thirled
to mass-murder, loveless, Christless.
Ye're at the killin still,
like your forebears, like the brute beasts
when they saa ye for the first time.
And this bleed stinks as it did on yon day
when brither said to brither, "Let's awa to the fields".
The cauld grip o yon echo is here and nou
in your ain day. Sons, forget the cloods o bleed
spootin fae the yirth, forget your faithers;
their tombs meissle awa in the mools,
the black birds, the wind, hap up their herts.

Owerset fae the Italian o Salvatore Quasimodo by Alastair Mackie

After the First Hard Rain

W. P. Anderson

She hobbles in pain. Each stair is an obstacle. He fusses at her side, offers to take the canes. She refuses with a shake of her head. The canes help anticipate the next step, the next steep drop. Barely a third of the way down, already gasping for breath, she sits. To sit she has only to lean back, so steep the decline, so tall each stair – like steps in the stone face of a pyramid.

The hospital beggar women, black shawls fluttering in the restive air, sidle closer to their motionless prey.

"For the love of God, share your good fortune." Uncomprehending, she raises her eyes to meet theirs.

"You're alive," one whispers. "You're leaving," rasps another. "You have a man."

"Leave her alone." He gives them each a gold-coloured coin as though sharing out cake. Seeing the look in her eyes he flushes and looks away. Rising stiffly, she resumes the descent, canes clicking hollowly against the quiet stone.

She stops, winded, halfway down.

"For the love of God, leave us *something*."

"I'm sorry," he says. She has already started down. They pause two thirds of the way to the bottom. Voices rise from a murmur to a sigh, "*...por el amor de Dios...*" She moves on. Near the bottom there is never any shade. The women are older and silent. Black dresses, slack at the breast. Seamed foreheads, seared like the bases of clay cooking pots. Long white hairs start from tresses the colour of raw yarn. Lips move soundlessly. An arm is raised slightly, bent at the elbow, suspended at the wrist by an unseen thread. The upturned palm is cupped and empty.

At the very bottom now, not so much as a withered arm is raised in supplication. She looks back to the tall, white building topping the pyramid steps. From where he stands the desolation in her face is hidden from him. The last time she wore that flowered cotton dress it clung tight to her body...she had long hair, and they had children. Now the dress hangs slack on a child with an old face and a skull wrapped in bandages.

Just short of the waiting taxi – he doesn't drive any longer – she stops at the last in a row of vendor's stands. For sale are small, clay flasks of cool water. Potters in her village used to make them. Reaching into the dry folds at her breast she extracts a 1000 *peso* note crumpled like a leaf, and exchanges it for a flask. He waits, telling the driver to start the meter. She removes the flask's cap, and breathes deeply. Moist clay: it smells of the earth after a hard rain. Unable to resist any longer she takes a bite from the lip of the flask. She savours the taste of clay as it fills her mouth. Looking up, she sees him watching her.

During the ride home he watches from the corner of his eye: she sniffs as if at a loaf of warm bread, and gnaws stealthily. Water and grit have spilled darkly onto the front of her dress. The taxi pulls up before the house. He looks at her anxiously: his little surprise now seems a cruel and gruesome trick. When she hears the baby... She will hear the baby any moment now.

But there is no scene, no explosion of grief or rancour. Her indifference, an absolute indifference, extends also to the infant. Only the clay pots animate her.

The maids stop coming. Soon clay rasps underfoot and the silent house smells of freshly-turned loam. She wanders in the empty bedrooms, pauses a moment beside the bunk beds and moves on.

Only as the child sickens does her interest in it kindle. Its respiration has become laboured. Breath rattles and clicks through its windpipe. She spends hours in its room, trying to feed it clay dissolved in milk. Often away, he does not understand. But the night the child dies he dreams, in another bed miles away, of a girl with his wife's voice singing lullabies to a barking pup...

Now she is alone and does not deny her growing appetite. There are so many pots. Those that remain intact seem more delicious than the ones she has begun to eat. Half-eaten pots litter the house.

She is drawn to the garden, drawn to the smell of flowers decaying in the earth. Day and night she lies in the parched brown garden, encircled by its high walls. She thinks of rain. She does not want to miss the smell of the earth after a hard rain. She lies on her back and waits, gnawing at a crumbling handful of dirt, keeping her strength up. She listens to the wind shifting dry leaves around the garden, hears them scraping against its walls.

The neighbours find her the morning after the first hard rain. Their dog has been barking. Either at her or at the black birds assembling on the high stone walls. She is lying on her back, naked, each hand filled with moist earth. By repeatedly spreading wide her arms and legs she has made an angel in the mud. Her eyes are closed. Her sun-blackened face is peaceful. Because her mouth is filled with soil – a rich, damp soil – not everyone present agrees that she is really smiling. The least sentimental prefer to see a rictus of death set in her cheeks. Yet it was one of these dispassionate souls who first claimed to have seen a tiny crop of fresh, white-flowered clover sprouting from her smile.

Gavin Ewart

Some Poems Complain

We are hating the rhymes
the steady dripping effect
like being hit on the head by a raindrop
at regular intervals

We are loathing the metrics
the tight smug stanzas
like smiling boxes

We want out
we want freedom
even rhythm disgusts us!

Edinburgh Closes (Festival Time)

In the clean uncluttered Closes
there are plates with patterned roses
and satin bows are plastered on the towels –
it's not like Bombay or Delhi,
they're not noisome, foul or smelly,
and the landladies are careful with their vowels.

There is Culture, there is Schooling,
and the television's ruling,
there's no hint of crime; it's squeamishness, not squalor.
There's no deviousness or dodging,
ladies offer genteel lodging
in exchange for English pound, or yen, or dollar.

But go back to 1830* –
dark, dangerous and dirty
they were then; and (what now might seem absurder)
Burke and Hare were drunk and active
and the Closes weren't attractive
except to those who contemplated murder!

*The very late 1820s, to be exact.

Cats and Owls

Cats and owls are fluffy,
cuddly as soft toys –
but when it comes right down to
all that macho hunting

an owl is one of the boys!

Cats that purr so softly
are noble, neat and nice –
but tell that to the rabbits,
tell that to the blackbirds,
tell that to the mice!

Cats and owls aren't friendly
all the bloody time –
the point of view's important;
and teeth and claws and talons
are a vole's eye view of crime!

Taunting a Philistine in 1936

You look to me the kind of prick
who's never been to Walberswick –
the kind of basic business vulture
who's never found at haunts of culture:
Bayreuth, Glyndebourne, Dartington Hall,
you've never heard of them at all!

National Gallery, the Tate –
you would rather masturbate.
The frilly knickers of a tart
are preferred to all High Art.
I'm a Muse, and you must see
you're not the kind of man for me!

Classical Comedies

What do they say about women?
That they're sometimes not very fair,
a spider in its lair,
too intriguing and tactical?
But at least they're always overwhelmingly practical.

All the best women know infallibly
exactly what should go where –
and she can put it there,
when she's the cooed-at and the doved one.
And how to smuggle a letter to the loved one!

However innocent, in romantic comedies
they love what is rich and rare,
walk with their bottoms bare
spiritually – they have their own intentions,
though there are things that no one ever mentions!

Bill Turner

Interlude

Waiting for you, I remembered the raccoons
braced on hind legs, forepaws on the bars,
importuning like depraved child actors
switching on pathos for the zoom lens.
I always meant to return to that zoo,
I recollected, while waiting for you.

Watching for you, I noticed those loose tiles
which I ought to fix before winter sets in.
Leaves keep scurrying into doorways, hasty
as under-the-wire refugees in search
of temporary shelter, yet already there's
one resentful neighbour out with a broom.

Listening for you, I caught snatches of music,
quickstep clicking of heels, and tired gears
protesting at unreasonable hills.
But the sparrows kept quarrelling over
the yellow cake crumbs I threw out at dawn,
and now the best part of the day has gone.

Writing to you, I pause in the middle
of a sentence to imagine you selecting
a word like a choice grape, before parted lips
follow through to a smile. I like waiting
for your reactions, watching for your frown,
listening for the quickening of your breath.

Getting one's act together

One drawback to the unicycle,
confides our street performer
to his passing throng,

is that it lacks both steering and brakes.
This he promptly demonstrates
by wildly veering

through a straggle of shoppers, since speed
and balance can reconcile
sober careering

with the wayward knack of a juggler.
Now the solo wheel wheedles
a quickstep shimmy

as he contrives to keep assorted
objects randomly whirling
in weird harmony.

All this is just the build-up, of course.
The real *tour de force* consists
of blazing torches

and of all things, a bright green apple.
Watch how those blistering fists
command spinning flames

as sweet Granny Smith intersperses
parabolas of dervish
abandon: the fork

gripped between teeth achieves a climax
with prongs impaling the fruit
while this crowd applauds.

So each one nervously devises
detours from mortality,
dangerous gambols.

Most wheeler-dealers stick with basics;
sound clubs, glittering contacts,
discreet name-dropping.

Just steady the wheel while I mount, please.
Oops! My sore thumb tingles. Now
I'm nearly ready.

Apple of my inner eye, you know why
this obstruction in my throat
still thrums for you.

Celebrating the Sandwich

Time spent on dining is gambling time squandered,
mused the fourth Earl of Sandwich as he pondered
his cards. "So bring me, good fellow, two slabs of bread
with prime ham and mustard between them," he said.

You gave a certain status to the fast food theme,
John Montagu, two hundred years ago;
you'd have fitted in well with our current regime.

Yet the sandwich nowadays is performance art,
convenience reconciled with gourmet dream:
one bite to charm the taste-buds from the start.

We've come a long way from the ploughman's lunch,
though cheese and pickles rate as *à la carte*
if you are moved to savour as you munch.

The secret's in proportions: I would swear
that to come between a gambler and his hunch
needs one part imagination, nine parts *flair!*

All sandwich sustenance, subtle or robust,
depends upon the sandwich maker's care.
Freshly sliced bread, buttered crust to crust,

offers unlimited scope for appetite.
The filling should be adequate, but must
not overwhelm the bread, or be too slight.

For sleight of hand is helpless to protect
a hasty filling, booby-trapped, which might,
on being nibbled, suddenly eject

an egg-white skid-lid, or stealthily ooze
mayonnaise down a gaping sleeve. I suspect
these are crises which nobody would choose.

As for the open sandwich, that sublime
nonsense of contradiction, I refuse
to look at one, like *sonnet without rhyme!*

In the first place, best to bake one's own bread
to ensure even texture; it's no crime
to cherish each particle on which you've fed.

I add malt and nutmeg to the flour in mine
before kneading the yeast in; jumping ahead,
the bouquet this exudes is nostril wine!

Now, my Designer Sandwich! This involves
avocado, tuna fillets, any fine
cheese, and the juice of half a lime. It solves

that transition point when parties decline
by revving up the inner gastric valves
of guests whose chatter has yawed to a whine.

The language of the sandwich can transcend
tongue-tied barriers. Its mission is benign.
The housewife's stand-by, the bachelor's friend,

it fills the gap between more routine meals.
Its popularity survives each trend,
and city gamblers snatch one between deals.

Homage to our National Cycle Museum

After cherubim straddling wheels of fire
and rumours of centaurs marauding through meadows
eventually a spindly virus of imagination
erupted and made manifest the bicycle.

How many cantankerous hobbyhorse contraptions
galumphed in the brimstone steam of the forge
before a hiccup between horseshoe and harrow
gave impetus to that compulsive treadle?

In Kirkpatrick MacMillan's prototype hulk
ploughbeam and spinning-jenny merge to convey
far more than the blacksmith lusted to achieve,
euphoric at a medley of grasshopper shadows.

From the lumbering bulk of it you can guess
how taking a bull by the horns inspired men
to steer by handlebars, yet left them saddled
with this mad urge to justify resemblances.

Spin-offs surround us: spidery fandangles
ogle iron scroll curlicues. Brass bedknobs
preside over skeletal racks and sprockets
like inquisitors of all faith in progress.

Now clutches of hunched skedaddlers surge round
competitive bends, spurring desperately on
as if despairing of catching the economy
before it takes off for outer space.

While wooden wheels dwindled to rubber and wire
the sparks that sprang from a particular anvil
continue to circuit as time is recycled.
Spokesmen, a penny-farthing for your thoughts.

Letters & Reviews

Dream State Continues...

Soutar Hoose
PERTH

Dear Joy,

Congratulations on your fine Ian Hamilton Finlay feature in *Chapman 78/79*, and on allowing Michael Hulse to reveal the extent of his prejudice in his review of *Dream State: The New Scottish Poets*, where he poses as "the only question", "whether there is such a thing as New Scottish Poetry (rather than poetry that happens to have been written by Scottish writers)." Easy as it may be to dismiss this as mere semantics, it is potentially an offensive denial of the distinctive nature of Scottish culture. It is not that his argument may, as Hulse suggests, "upset a nationalist who admits the truth of the observation", it is likely to "upset" Scottish-based people who refute his highly subjective "truth". The crux is contained in Hulse's misreading of the two lines by W.N. Herbert he quotes:

There is no passport to this country
it exists as a quality of the language

By this, he assumes that Herbert is "plainly not thinking of ... poets who write in Gaelic ... nor of the versions of Scots".

Only ignorance based on a wilfully selective reading of the text can explain such cursory dismissal of the contributions in Gaelic and Scots. Indeed, his review is a perfect example of the complex identified elsewhere as "metro-parochial xenophobia" (*Edinburgh Review* 91: 'An Attitude Problem Based in London', Murdo Macdonald, 1994), as betrayed by the following statement:

The fact is that most of the poetry here is written in the English which is assumed to be the proper vehicle for universal currency and most of it differs from poetry south of the border in little more than its place names.

He doesn't say who makes this grand assumption, nor consider that there may be other vehicles towards "universal currency". What about poetry in other great languages of the world – are these, like Scots and Gaelic, to be considered improper? And what about the inherent poetry of placenames themselves, the ability of names like Suilven to conjure an image in the mind of the reader familiar with the place?

The idea that poetry in this "proper vehicle" gains "strength" because "these poets feel at ease on a larger stage" is laughable – there is nothing to indicate "disease" on the part of poets who do not use the "proper vehicle". This suggestion echoes the old attitude, which ought to be long buried, that Scots is corrupted English. The decision to write in Scots or Gaelic is not a denial of English but an affirmation of Scotland's other tongues. And any performer will tell you that the intimate atmosphere of the small space can be more challenging than the great auditorium, where the gulf between audience and performer acts like a protective moat. Reading a poem to one person who knows you, knows where the poem comes from and why, is a more rigorous test than addressing a thousand strangers for whom you are an exotic migratory bird. Those writers who do not polarise towards the cosy insularity of a metropolitan poetic elite, but who remain in their community as working writers, have often had a much harder time of it.

As might be expected, Carol Ann Duffy, whose time in Scotland was limited to roughly her first eight years, is Hulse's star witness. In the four lines quoted:

It makes me sick. My soul is not a vest
spattered with wee black marks. Miracles and
               shamrocks
and transubstantiation are all my ass.
For Christs' sake, do not send your kids to Mass.

Hulse thinks "it's Larkin we hear... behind these lines" – again the assumption, the appropriation of the "we" to suggest that his view is concurrent with the majority's . He may well hear Larkin, because the cultural matrix he inhabits would programme him to do so, and it may well be that Duffy *is* deliberately Larkining about. But to assume that there is no Scottish context for these lines is simply wrong. For instance, Scottish readers of *Dream State* may see, like myself, the tongue-in-cheek Lochee Catholicism of Michael Marra in this extract from Duffy's work. But then maybe Hulse has never heard of Marra.

Hulse's second witness is Don Paterson, who also has lived much of his life in the south. The quotation Hulse uses to illustrate the placelessness of Paterson's writing is again mistaken – for a Scottish audience, the fact that is it a "John Martyn Album mumbling through the speakers" is significant. Martyn, like Alex Harvey and other seventies Scottish rock stars, represents a link between the familiar world and contemporary "alternative" culture. But maybe Hulse doesn't know that Martyn originates from Shawlands.

In summation, Hulse states that:

> ... what's good in the poems in *Dream State* has no more to do with Scotland than with California. I wish we could put this boring stuff about nations aside when we gather poems. No doubt the answer must be that a nation denied nationhood must feel the need more acutely; but even as I respect that, I still have to add that I can't for the life of me see what it's got to do with poetry.

Here he makes the error of equating place with nation, nationhood with state. Though it may not have an assembly, Scotland exists as a particular context, with distinctive institutions as detailed in Lindsay Paterson's recent *The Autonomy of Modern Scotland*. The interpretations of the view from Scotland are diverse, and expressed in many forms – linguistically, through the use of Gaelic, Scots *and* English. The more distinctive linguistic forms cannot be excised as extraneous to the argument, for the continued existence of Gaelic and Scots, in spite of erosion, is the background against which all writing by Scots in English must be set. This is the message in the lines by Herbert quoted above, which brings to mind Lewis Grassic Gibbon's assertion that:

> ...however the average Scots writer believes himself to be Anglicized, his reaction upon the minds of the intelligent English reader is curiously similar to that produced by the English poems of Dr. Rabindranath Tagore... it is as though the writer did not *write* himself, but *translated* himself. ...Often the Scots writer is quite unaware of this essential foreignness in his work; more often, seeking an adequate word or phrase he hears an echo in an alien tongue that would adorn his meaning with a richness, a clarity and a conciseness impossible in orthodox English. That echo is from Braid Scots...

Though the breakdown of "orthodox English" may have ameliorated the intensity of the opposition between Scots and English for Scottish writers, and while the aspiration to create a "universal" poetry is worthy enough, there is an increased awareness throughout the 'English-speaking world' that writing gleans much of its vitality and colour from localised, idiomatic expression, not universal blandishments about the human condition.

Hulse's apparent ignorance of the Scottish scene may be telling in relation to his later comments in the same review on *Sixty Women Poets*, and suggest that it is by means of many tiny recognitions that the commonality of any group is established. Perhaps the outsider cannot be expected to notice, or indeed value, these. Clearly he is drawing a parallel between "the gender ghetto" and "Scottish nationalism". But once again the appropriation of that royal "we" in the phrase "Aren't we past all that now?" sticks in the craw - he may be tired of it, but many of us choose to continue to live, with dignity, in our "ghetto", because it is our place, where we belong.

Hulse's argument dulls entirely when, from the short biographical note that attributes to him co-editorship of *The New Poetry*, the glint of a personal axe requiring the grindstone shines. Yes, the uninitiated reader may think such a broad-based title for his own anthology concurs with his argument against locality. A pity then that his is simply an allusion to Al Alvarez's 1962 volume, punting in the shallow stream of the Anglopoetic tradition to create a further narrow definition of the 'canon'.

R A Jamieson

The Politics of Language

How Late it Was, How Late, James Kelman, Secker and Warburg, £14.99; *Foreign Parts*, Janice Galloway, Jonathan Cape, £14.99 and £5.99; *Music, In a Foreign Language*, Andrew Crumey, Dedalus, £7.99; *Last Lesson of the Afternoon: A Satire*, Christopher Rush, Canongate Press, £9.99

At one point in James Kelman's *How Late it was, How Late*, Sammy, the ex-convict who finds he has gone blind after the police have detained and beaten him up following a heavy drinking session, attempts to describe his predicament to the DSS authorities. The report of his first interview with them causes difficulties. So, he is interviewed again:

What's entered here is the phrase 'they gave me a doing', and it's entered expressly as a quotation. But it's a colloquialism and not everyone who deals with yer claim will understand what it means. I felt that it was fair to use physical beating by way of an exposition but if you would prefer something else... is there anything else ye can think of?

It was a fight.

Pardon?

Look, what does it say?

They gave ye a doing.

Can I change it?

No, I'm sorry, but ye can add to it for purpose of clarification, if ye wish to clarify what you mean then ye can do

Sammy rubbed at his chin, moving the flesh at the jawbone. He should have shaved, it was a mistake no to. He sniffed then said:

They were using physical restraints.

What is significant about this exchange, and the entire novel focuses on how Sammy learns to cope with his misfortune, is that it shows how for Kelman language is the battlefield in which people like Sammy, marginalised by the well-off and the manipulatively articulate, have to survive. Even Sammy's physical gestures confirming he hasn't shaved reveal that he knows he's at a disadvantage. The bureaucrat portrayed here may or may not be well-meaning, but the reader cannot be sure one way or another, because she too is constrained by language, that of officialdom. Before she can help Sammy at all, if that is her intention, she needs to transform his language into someone else's, namely the language of those who decide (very impersonally mind you) how people like Sammy should be treated. Sammy himself surrenders, even if with a hint of irony, to this kind of language, hence his use of the euphemistic phrase, "physical restraint".

As for Sammy's frequent resort to four-letter expletives, which has provoked such critical antagonism against Kelman, he can be highly poignant in his use of them. Here is one of Sammy's philosophical observations: "Folk take a battering but, they do; they get born and they get brought up and they get fuckt. That's the story; the cot to the fucking funeral pyre." Such sombre eloquence about the essence of life is reminiscent of the following lines from *Waiting for Godot*: "They give birth astride of a grave, the light gleams an instant, then it's night once more."

Beckett's speaker is Pozzo and, as it happens, only seconds before uttering "one day I went blind." Kelman's achievement, resented so much by some, is that he forces the reader to perceive the world as Sammy does. It is precisely *how Sammy speaks*, indeed how he *must* speak, which defines his world. But Kelman can be extremely prickly in the twists and turns of his irony about language. Sammy himself, after all, tells his son near the end of the novel, "I swear too much don't I!"

A zone of language more accommodating to fleeting impressions, bitterly painful memories, and the strains of friendship is evident in *Foreign Parts*, its territory staked out by Cassie and Rona, two Scottish women driving through Northern France. To call the journey allegorical would be to oversimplify Janice Galloway's technique of revelation, but the journey does resonate with implied questions about what kind of Europe we live in. Certainly historical echoes are more than hinted at in the landscape. Readers may recall the "auld alliance", or William of Normandy's conquest of England, which eventually affected Scotland as well. Not least, Cassie and Rona drive through First World War battlefields. Snippets of tourist brochures, and an old postcard from Rona's grandfather, a casualty of war, in fact, enrich the pattern of the narrative.

As with Kelman's Sammy, the reader gets to know Cassie and Rona extremely well, almost intimately. Galloway achieves this primarily through a "pointillist" style which evokes the counterpoint of their fugitive thoughts (very different from conventional stream-of-consciousness) and disjointed fragments of conversation as the two friends continually size each other up, and reflect on their past experiences, especially the men in their lives. But if Galloway's rendering of their relationship is undeniably sensitive, the broader implications of *Foreign Parts* raise it to an even higher level of artistry. One key to its artistry lies in a passage about the evanescence of memory when linked to artistic appreciation in the context of a touristic jaunt:

A bunch of complaisant angels hanging out of the sky to stab a dragon and baby dragon. Smug buggers. They only had the German version of the guidebook so I had to guess what things were about. I bought these post-cards because they didn't allow you to take photos. I thought it was a great idea: not being able to distance through a lens, you'd really need to take the thing for what it was, its existence in the moment etc. And it was beautiful. I remember telling myself it *was* beautiful, awesome, strange. But all the time I knew it wouldn't be as beautiful as it would be when I was somewhere else, remembering. And that it was equally possible I wouldn't be able to remember a single stitch of the bloody thing unless I bought this. You don't remember just by telling yourself you should, by sheer act of will. You don't get to pick and choose. The same way you don't get to forget. Memory. A bastard really. A complete bastard.

Rona's musings, provoked by a medieval "Tapestry of the Apocalypse", reveal how out of touch Europeans have become with their past. Her observations on memory, moreover, are worthy of Proust. But where for Proust memory is redemptive, for Galloway it is "a bastard". So, what survives around us, even the most wonderful works of art, is not sufficient to impress our memories. Instead, we frantically need to photograph and film everything we see. The historical past is just not real enough for most people. Just as Kelman's novel portrays, according to Alasdair Gray in *The Scotsman* last Christmas, a Britain many would prefer to ignore, Galloway's reveals a Europe too alienated from its own roots.

Set in England under a Communist regime, but having little in common with Orwell's *Nineteen Eighty-Four*, Andrew Crumey's *Music, In a Foreign Language* focuses on a different friendship, that between a philandering physicist and a gay historian. The woman they are both involved with completes the triangle. Heavily influenced by Calvino and Kundera, the novel, Crumey's first, has one of those narrators who feels it necessary to remind the reader that this is a work of fiction. Crumey, however, allows the core story of love, betrayal and political dissidence under "genteel English Communism" enough room to entertain in conventional thriller manner. A mathematician himself, his novel is elegantly mathematical in its ingenious plot and narrative, and highly suggestive about the music of Beethoven and Bach. Highly readable, but its language too studiously neutral in accent.

The same criticism cannot be levelled at Christopher Rush's *Last Lesson of the Afternoon*. His language has very different failings, it is far too ripe, overblown and aggressively scatological. Alan Taylor in *Scotland on Sunday* has praised the "sandblasting brilliance of its venomous attack" on the education system. He has also accurately described the novel as a "bawdy autobiographical monologue" by Campbell MacKay, "an English teacher at the fag end of his career." I cannot agree, however, about the "sandblasting brilliance" of Rush's attack on the education system. My problem with MacKay is that I find him too masochistic to be a convincing standard-bearer for literary values. Rush seems very naive in assuming that satirical indignation demands relentless scatology. It is very evident, moreover, that Rush has learned little from James Kelman's very different novel about a teacher at the end of his tether, *A Disaffection*.

Mario Relich

Righteous Pirates

Klaonica: Poems for Bosnia, ed Ken Smith & Judi Benson, Bloodaxe, £7.95; *Under Cover*, ed Colin Nicholson & Jane Ogden Smith, Mainstream, £6.99; *The Stone Sleeping Bag*, Douglas Lipton, Mariscat, £5.95; *Cardboard Troy*, William Oxley, Stride, £5.95; *Tube Shelter Perspective*, Richard Price, Southfields Press, £A

Both *Klaonica* and *Under Cover* are anthologies designed to raise money for good causes. Sales of *Klaonica* will be donated to *Feed the Children*, to relieve suffering in Bosnia. Sales of *Under Cover* will be donated to *Shelter*, the charity dedicated to helping homeless people.

Klaonica – Serbo-Croat for slaughterhouse, abattoir, butchery – is not a comfortable read. Although there has been criticism of the ethics of poets uninvolved in the suffering in Bosnia writing poems about it, and such poems are included in this book, one only occasionally senses a descent towards uninvolved voyeurism, or poets are feigning responses so as to be anthologised. *Klaonica* is prefaced by a chilling quotation by Ivo Andric, about the possibility that the Balkan peoples may have been poisoned forever with the spirit of revenge – one is reminded of Irish poet Brendan

Kenelly's stunning poem, 'The Grudge' – and the book concludes with an extract from the ecologically-wise speech of Chief Seattle of the Suquamish to the United States President in 1854. Between these two, set like entrance and exit, the reader enters a charred forest of present savagery and radiant reminiscence, political analysis and poetic fable. A small proportion of the poems are by Bosnian writers, translated by Mario Susko; the rest are by British writers, with one or two Americans and Europeans. The work of the Bosnian poets is understandably grim, but among them is an astonishingly benevolent poem, confirming poetry's right to the non-stock response, by Marko Vesovic; 'Clearing Up', in the aftermath of an assault in the "cruelly beautiful" day, the poet feels "That good threatened evil with an inescapable/ checkmate,/ and that everyone would be issued a visa to paradise/ and that we, kinder than Francis of Assisi himself, wished/ even to call a horse-whip brother!"

Some of the most effective poems recount peacetime memories of Yugoslavia: Tom Pow laments the village "where once/ they spoke with such eloquence/the ripe language of pears." Roy Fisher grimly recognises normal life being "nothing more/than a counter devised for murderers to bargain with."

The issue of the relation of poetry to such extreme experience is hardly new. After World War II the Eastern European Anti-poets wrote poetry whose purpose, they said, was to avoid giving pleasure. Verbally stripped down, it was bleak in the extreme. To its credit, there is little 'pleasure', except in harrowed memory, in *Klaonica*. Poetry in its rhythms and patterns is essentially of life, and the energies that lead to wars are horribly of life also. That uneasy paradox is the undercurrent running through many of the poems in this charring book.

Under Cover, a mix of often superb short stories and poetry, is less relentless. Homelessness is simply implied in many pieces here, and its variations investigated: homelessness as estrangement, for one. I preferred the prose to the verse, though fine poems are included: among others, a sharp, clean piece about homeless war-veterans, by William Neill; a dark memory of the drowning of kittens by Stewart Conn; and a genuinely humble piece by Derick Thomson about standing with the dispossessed in a post-office queue. Alasdair Gray and James Kelman contribute stories which fascinatingly investigate the labourer-foreman relationship, and which will provoke memories in anyone who has ever worked on a building site or similar situation. Some writers examine what happens when the worlds of the dispossessed and those more fortunate abrade: Dilys Rose's fine piece consists of alternating interior monologues by a Social Worker and her "client"; in Moira Burgess' 'The Privacy Switch', a young couple pretend to be house-hunting and are shown round a flat by the occupiers, the man scornful and unsympathetic, the woman more open, to the couple's plight when revealed. And there is hilarity too: Jeff Torrington's 'Getting There!' is a loony sub-Conan Doyle romp, and John McGill's 'Doktor Weitundbreit' has a mad Doctor searching for, and finding, a speaking sheep on Shetland, a story which works on several levels and has a sting in the tail.

Douglas Lipton's *The Stone Sleeping Bag*, tastefully produced by Mariscat Press, opens with the sequence 'The Flora and Fauna of an Independent Scotland', lively sardonic monologues in Scots, only occasionally predictable, spoken by everything from great skuas to midges to wild strawberries. Contrasting markedly is the central sequence, dedicated to victims of Lockerbie, 'Songs For a Falling Angel', in which Lipton attempts to resurrect the universal impersonality of some medieval English poems; a note tells that one lyric, 'Processional' was based on the 7th-century Anglian poem 'The Dream of the Rood'. Though I would have liked more rhyme, the heightened world-embracing impersonality of the sequence is refreshing in these self-absorbed times. Among the shorter poems, 'Ceol Mor Outside Barlinnie' is a haunting poem about the "landlocked island" of the prison, its windows "grid-ironed to repel/ the righteous pirates of the outside world/ from boarding." Among my favourite pieces, though, is 'Sea Dog', a lovely mix of wistfulness and humour dedicated to Tess, whose nose "is a black sea anemone", and who has "the smell of starfish/about her toes..."

There is a headlong energy and boisterousness about William Oxley's *Cardboard Troy* which makes you well-disposed towards the

poet without necessarily taking to all of his poems. Some have portentous titles like 'The Wordless Glory' or 'The Inner Tapestry', but one is carried along by his driving rhythms and the skewed craft of the enterprise. In 'Cardboard Troy' about homeless men there is no lack of empathy, but Oxley does not drown the subjects in pity – Boxo, Fang and Bones make the best of an awful situation and Oxley acknowledges their individuality and refuses to make them prey to their condition. 'One in the Eye', another outstanding poem, recounts a schoolboy fight when the young Oxley, sneaking up to thrust a handful of snow down the back of a girl's dress, receives a snowball in the eye meant for her – she ducks. The poem mingles reality, humour and morality, concluding: "I never learnt a lesson like it at school."

Richard Price's *Tube Shelter Perspective* is described by the blurb as a "phantasmagoria" of the London Underground. Though Price can show a gift for the startling image, the much underestimated 'ordinary' reader would only be occasionally engaged by these often obscure pages. Price's previous publication, *Sense and a Minor Fever*, at least contained more comprehensible work and shareable sentiment. I can see no point to this, for instance, which, untitled, takes up a full page:

Through an exit a fireman with a concourse round him
        steps back.
Our carriages don't
           coagulate.

Price's best work occurs when there is an emotional centre to what he has to say, counterpointed by his often dry tone. That is true in *Tube Shelter Perspective* also, but the curious poignance that marked the best of *Sense and a Minor Fever* is largely, and unfortunately, absent.   *Gerry Cambridge*

Theatre Roundup

Given that the Scottish Arts Council's power to shape one is circumscribed by lack of cash, is it mainly journalists who think in terms of an 'agenda' for Scottish Theatre? If so does this make debate on the subject any less valid? The major agenda theatre directors follow is that which will fill their theatres, while actors have their career agenda to worry about. We all have

our jobs to do but a bit of reality on this subject would save theatre criticism from some of the savage subjectivity and hot air to which it is prone. Literary critics seldom castigate Scottish publishers for not following some national masterplan, rather they assess how well any given book accomplishes what it sets out to do.

Of course critics should do what they can (sadly not much) to encourage the optimum conditions for exciting Scottish work, and certainly should not restrict themselves to the self-important distribution of good and bad marks. But as agendas discussions seem to mean so little to the theatre-going public, it should be remembered that debate on 'whither Scottish theatre?' lines is only sensible as long as we do not deceive ourselves that it makes much difference to the day-to-day pressures of this branch of the entertainment business.

Not that there has been over much whithering in what has been an interesting few months. The National Theatre Campaign hit the ground running in the post-Festival season with their well-attended *Stage Secrets* – rehearsed readings, successfully designed to showcase the gems of the Scottish repertoire. Although far from negative in conception, the season's main achievement was to refute one of the sloppier arguments against the National Theatre idea, that it would be stuck for decent material.

In their short and sweet pamphlet *The Scottish Stage*, published in October, the campaign laid out its stall and with rare political generosity, identified some of the common objections to the idea. This one will run and run in pursuit of the tantalisingly visible, but still elusive, critical mass, even if the vital support of Scotland's handful of true theatrical visionaries and leaders is still deafeningly absent.

Honours of the late summer and autumn belong to the Citizens Theatre, where we can assume that the 'whither?' question is seldom posed. This was a remarkable series of rarities and new dramatisations, attacked as if they were hoary old theatrical staples in need of spicing up. With *The Aspern Papers, The Father, Private Lives, The Milk Train Doesn't Stop Here Anymore, A Taste of Honey, Gertrude Stein*, the common thread was an uncompromisin, lurid theatricality flecked with wonderfully precise and tender performances from the self-sufficient resident company.

Elsewhere in Scotland, many truffles were there to be found, but needed a bit more snuffling out, to use an appropriate metaphor for Communicado's *A Place With the Pigs*, in which Gerry Mulgrew made a beast of himself as Soviet Army deserter hiding out in a sty. Athol Fugard's dramatic poetry of self–liberation soared in Kenny Glenaan's production, which also featured an understated gem of a performance from Ann Louise Ross.

Glenaan was also responsible for another highlight of the past few months, James Kelman's *One Two – Hey*, further evidence in the case that could be made for this writer as a true heir to Beckett's precision, thoroughness and profound elegance as a dramatist. Using non-actors and blues musicians, the production had a different taste to anything else on offer, and signalled that Soundhouse Productions may well be a force to be reckoned with.

Although more wide-ranging and high-stepping in literary style the same sort of poetic integrity and intelligence were also evident in David Greig's work. In *Europe*, his play for the Traverse, the 20-something Edinburgh writer worked out his obsessions with Mitteleuropa and the human fallout from its seismic convulsions. Greig followed this up a few months later with Suspect Cultures's production of *One Way Street*, another ambitious attempt to show how history happens to people.

Stephen Greenhorn's self-imposed discipline of writing a tragedy resulted in *The Salt Wound*, directed by Jim Culleton for 7:84. The story of a fisherman who defies his mother's premonitions to go to sea, it was an unusual play for the 1990s, but the trick of timelessness it achieved showed skill. Too self-consciously teeth-gnashing to be truly moving, but it had undeniable power and verve.

Other stand-out productions of the past few months include TAG's witty and well-spoken production of *As You Like It* by Tony Graham which blazed a trail around Scotland on tour. Graham played around with the play's gender-bending to hilarious effect, and pulled off the rare feat of showing Shakespeare as the all-ages playwright he is. Also distinguishing themselves in the Shakespearian sphere were Eve Jamieson's *Merchant of Venice* for the Brunton in Musselburgh, and Richard Baron's *Comedy of Errors* at Perth, both of which were full of surprises in their textual interpretation.

Public indifference to critical beefs was demonstrated beyond doubt with Bill Bryden's *The Big Picnic*, a million pound extravaganza inspired by Govan's experience of the 'war to end all wars'. No-one denied that Bill Dudley's transformation of Harland & Wolff shipyard was a spectacular feat of design pyrotechnics, though the dramatic bones on which this pageant hung were critically condemned as feeble in the extreme. 'No script and no politics' was the gist of the reaction, though the contempt of the Scottish press was in direct relation to the adulation of their English colleagues and the volume of the attending audience. Judged on the criteria above, this mega-event was the theatrical equivalent of a Runrig concert; loud, technically lavish, and hootingly pompous. If the public liked it, it had to be because the public prefers to be overwhelmed rather than made to think. The fools!

The growth of the co-production ideas as a way around the theatre's current poverty-factor resulted in notably strong Dundee Rep/Royal Lyceum productions of *Dancing at Lughnasa* and *Death & the Maiden*. Apparently these resource pooling ventures are not the money savers one might think, but any attempt to breach the fractured state of Scottish theatre has to be welcome.

Another more original and ambitious form of co-production was Boilerhouse's rave-induced *Headstate*, by Irvine Welsh, devised in co-operation with the Theatre Workshop, Aberdeen's Lemon Tree, Paisley Arts Centre and Glagow's Tramway, which forced this writer to heat his rude words about this company's strung-out theatrics. Tam Dean Burn's performance as a pimp and drugdealer was one of the most effective yet from this always mesmerising performer.

John McGrath's long cherished intention of putting Neil Gunn's *The Silver Darlings* surfaced in a fine production by Wildcat that circumvented the problem of putting a novel of this scale and thematic grandeur on the stage as well as any could have, though ironically it worked better in smaller spaces than the large ones. Seen at a distance from a large auditorium, its attempts at expressing the all-encompassing nature effects of the novel were somewhat muted, though in its central performance by Kevin McKidd as Finn was an extraordinarily charismatic professional debut.

Staying with symbolic treatments of the briny, Benchtours triumphed with a contemporary version, Salman Rushdie's *Haroun and the Sea of Stories*, a wildly inventive fantasy on the victory of free expression of the imagination, which Rushdie, present at the first night of the tour at the Traverse, still hopes will become a reality. The strength of this production was its ability to blur the boundaries between the child–mind and the adult, achieving a universal encompassing myth.

Finally, the bad news of the season was the withdrawal of the Scottish Arts Council's grant to the Brunton Theatre in Musselburgh on the sadly familiar grounds that sustaining assistance to a third theatre in Lothian was no longer economically feasible. That the Brunton company's future hangs in the balance is all the more regrettable given the strength of much of their recent work under director Robin Peoples, like Stewart Thomas's wartime nostalgia-fest *I'll be Seeing You*... which opened only weeks before the announcement. East Lothian District Council's generosity will be further taxed if the community is to continue to get the benefits it has learned to expect from a vital local resource.

Colin Donald

Pamphleteer

Some pamphleteer items belie their stapled exterior and contain treasures within like *Sex–Magic–Poetry–Cornwall: A Flood of Poems* by Peter Redgrove. This is an excellent selection of poetry and an extensive essay on the themes and theories of this unusual poet by Jeremy Robinson. Redgrove is unusual in that his poetry ranges outside of himself and connects not just with nature and its mysteries but with other people, particularly women. All those who get irritated by the self-centred tenor of most poetry check this out (£6.95 Crescent Publishing, 18 Chaddsley Road, Kidderminister, DY10 3AD).

Heartland (£3.50 Envoi Poets, Pen Ffordd, Newport, Dyfed, SA42 0QT) by James Deahl brings to life the Canadian countryside:

By late April the rains cease
rivers return to old channels

leaving pools that reflect
fresh green buds.

Under spring constellations
winds sweep the great oaks;
we walk near dark waters
with no need to speak.

Interesting to collectors of 'little known facts' the area of Canada Deahl writes about was settled by United Empire Loyalists who moved to Canada after the American Revolution, starting Anglican churches and Orange Lodges.

Further back in time *Perceptions of the Picts* by Anna Ritchie (Groam House Museum, High St Rosemarkie, IV10 8UF £4.50) is a readable and well-illustrated traul through the stereotypes and myths about the Picts. *The 1820 Rising: The Radical War* by James Halliday (Scots Independent, 51 Cowane St, Stirling, FK8 1JW £2.50) is a handy filler-in of the history behind illfated Hardie and Baird of Kelman's play. Both were sentenced to be hung and beheaded in Stirling for their part in the rising which started with the post-Waterloo discontent and weavers strike. Hardly a pamphleteer item at all – *The Paisley Poets: A Critical Reappraisal of their Work and Reputation* edited by James & McCrae contains edited lectures given as part of the Paisley 500 celebrations. It includes Donald Low on Burns, Mary Ellen Brown on Robert Tannahill – the weaver poet, and Konrad Hopkins on duality in Willam Sharp/Fiona MacLeod and John Wilson/Christopher North. (£2.99 Paisley Libraries / Paisley Univeristy)

The Poets' Quair (£2) published by the Moray District Library is the result of the Poet's Quair Competition, judged by the late Jessie Kesson. The winning entries attest to a heartening mix of Scots and English with the added bonus of Kesson's poems reproduced from *Chapman* giving another audience a chance to sample them. Grampian Community Education (£1.50) have published their first collection of writings culled from their over 50's class. *Ponderings* has a mix of poetry, fiction and reminiscence, largely in Scots

Short Circuits is a haiku sized collection of haiku's by Ken Morgan. (50p from author at 55 Haywood Court, Tenby Dyfed)

Trees are picked clean,
Ironclad November days:
Invisible sun.

Lapwing Publications (1 Ballysillan Drive, Belfast, BT14 8HQ) has produced a series of pamphlets, £2 each. *Sex, Rectitude & Loneliness* by James Simmonds has too much prose masquerading as poetry, and too much therapy masquerading as writing. In contrast, Desmond O'Grady's *My Fields This Springtime* is a reply to Derek Mahon's *A Sea in Winter*. It has great range both geographically and historically. O'Grady's immersion in a community of writers Irish and foreign has enriched his work whereas Simmonds speaks of its lack of history and connections. *The Only Ankles for Midges to Bite* by Ranald MacDonald, which sadly has no title poem, ranges round the themes of nature and Christianity. *No Surrender Castlecauldfield* by Ray Givans meditates on the significance of language and place names. Sabine Wichert in *Miranda* traces the otherness of exile and captures moments of clarity in a deft way.

> ... when winter
>
> comes, I shall be unprepared –
> and you ask me why I always
>
> Walk with my hands swinging openly
> by my side: I have to be ready
>
> for sudden changes from any
> direction, as I also always
>
> select with great care where
> I sit: the corner is best
>
> for defence...

Brown by Fred Johnstone is a bleak journey into the interior of a Belfast English teacher who develops a passion for one of his pupils.

Moving back across the water Neruda Press (51 Allison Street, Glasgow) have published a small collection of Rab Fulton's poetry *Revelation Rap* (£2). Fulton has rightly received much praise for his energetic and modern use of Scots. Grabbin it bi the heid an intae the 20th century an oot rural idyls an ither fantasies. Grab the *Revelation Rap* to read one of the better younger poets in Scotland. *A Laddie Looks at Leith* by Jim Blaikie is also in Scots but the poems are in nostalgic mode looking back at past times. As the author admits, it's a sobering thought when your memories become part of Social History. (£3 Hobby Press 12 Drum Brae Walk, Edinburgh, EH4 8DG)

From Raunchland Publications *The Man With the Staccato Brain* by John Mingay. Raunchland have been publishing these well designed attractive booklets for ten years. Mingay's pared down poetry is well complimented by Bill McKechnie's illustrations. (2 Henderson Street, Kingseat, Dunfermaline, Fife, KY12 0TP, £2)

Simon Darrragh is a poet plumber in Greece whose droughts leave more time for literary pursuits. Hearing Eye (Box 1, 99 Torriano Ave, London, NW5 2RX) have published a short pamphlet of his poems. *Poems from Alonnisos* gutter and spark but I don't think (despite the drought) that he has quite found the flame. Troika 1 from Scratch Press (Poetry as if it mattered) contains the work of 3 poets. Paul Donnelly 'Learning to Panic'

> Some nights
> I wake up wondering
> how thoroughly I've read
> Surrealist Poetry In English,
> a cold sweat for company,
> when I know I should be concerned
> about the state of my record collection:
> it's already the nineties
> and I have nothing
> by Wild Man Fisher.

One of those things... *Troika 1* also has poetry by John Duffy in Scots and English. His 'Ainjil' on the Fall is wonderful.(£5, 9 Chestnut Road, Eaglescliffe, Stockton-on-Tees, TS16 0BA)

Trout Minus 1 (£1 to Bill Douglas, 9 Halkshill Drive, Largs, KA30 9PD) is another threesome of poets. However they lacked the certain something and magic coupling of words to make poetry.*Object Permanence* is a new magazine which describes itself as having a bias towards experimental/Modernist work. Recent issues has included work by Edwin Morgan, Richard Price, WN Herbert, TA Clark, Peter Finch, and Gael Turnbull. Its production values are growing issue by issue and is worth picking up a copy (subscriptions £7.50, single copies £2.50, to Peter Manson, flat3/2, 16 Ancroft St, Glasgow, G20 7HU)

Finally if the dreich new year is getting you down I suggest a subbie to *The Angry Corrie* an irreverent and barbed (or cramponed?) hill-walking fanzine. Yes, when DTP technology was invented this is what it was going to liberate – let a thousand fanzines bloom, not another thousand badly written poems chucked in the face of an indifferent public.

The White Paper, *The Scottish Hills and How to Make Lots and Lots of Money out of Them*, was introduced at a time when... the beleagured Scottish radicals were too thinly spread & as usual too busy fighting amongst themselves to give this Paper the attention it deserved. George Galloway was unavoidably abroad in Italy renegotiating his contract with Versace. The editors of *The Angry Corrie*, by this time a samizdat publication, still had 20 years of their sentence to serve on the Penal Colony of Barra. The King of Thailand had written to the Prime Minister, Sir Michael Howard, asking for clemency on their behalf...

What chance we *don't* get OFHILL the consumers watchdog of the privatised hillside? The lack of access to our hills is a national disgrace. *The Angry Corrie* is available from all good outdoor shops and House 48, 170 Sandifield Road, Glasgow G5 0DL £1 single issue, £12.50 sub + T-shirt.

Catalogue

The New Companion to Scottish Culture, edited by David Daiches, republished by Polygon, undoubtedly fills a real need, but I forget where Olga Wojtas noted omissions in the literary section of the first version of this still insufficiently revised book. A cursory glance at the entry for William Soutar reveals nothing later than 1959, though much has happened since. Derick Thomson's *The Companion to Gaelic Scotland*, (Gairm) likewise revises a seasoned reference work in a handsomely illustrated edition.

Chapman was startled by news from valued poet Jenny Robertson that she would be living in what was insufficiently briefly Leningrad. Her *A Season in St. Petersburg* gets inside the city and manages to fight off both the tourist brand and the current press brand of cliché: valuable, Lion Publishing, Peter's Way, Sandy Lane West, Oxford OX4 5HG. Forest Books, 20 Forest View, Chingford, London E4 7AY, present possible successors of poets who got known when oppression rather than disorder was the cliche for Eastern Europe. *Contemporary Macedonian Poetry* tr. Ewald Osers, is of the quality one expects on seeing that venerable translator's name. Some mightily impressive items can be found too in *Young Poets of a New Poland* tr. Donald Pirie. From the Bulgarian Elisaveta Bagryana's *Penelope of the Twentieth Century*, has in Brenda Walker's versions a remarkable edge. *Cheerleader for a Funeral*, from the Romanian of Nina Cassian, has less force, perhaps because of the shortness of the poems and different needs in translating them. Blaga Dimitrova's *The Last Rock Eagle*, a third Brenda Walker translation, demonstrates that this translator does vary voice. All three poets sound different, nay distinctive. *The Day Tito Died*, contemporary short stories from Slovenia, £8.95, concludes an interesting Forest Walk that might be continued by reference to The Women's Press, who add *Marble Skin* to their books by Croatian novelist Slavenka Drakulic. There are also poems from the Croatian in Desmond O'Grady's 600 page *Trawling Tradition*, University of Salzbur. Forty years' translation work is represented by Caedmon, Archilocus, Abu Nuwas, Lorca, in a well-organised presentation. Bunting has been mentioned in these pages as an influence on O'Grady's verse.

A second volume of George Davie's essays on the Scottish Enlightenment, *A Passion for Ideas*, comes from Polygon at £8.50 and concentrates more on philosophy *pur* than did the first. There is even, as was once said of a Julian Barnes novel, a rejoinder to Derrida. Fionn MacColla's *Move Up, John*, Canongate, has required much work from editor, John Herdman, incorporating such substantial set-pieces as the *Scottish Noel* in what was planned as an exploration of the Scottish Reformation by a man with too big a bee in his bonnet about that theme. The lack of curates in Presbyterian Scotland maybe deflates the egg cliché so apt here. Ian Hamilton QC in *A Touch of Treason*, Neil Wilson Publishing, reveals why he is so esteemed as a man, despite a lifetime's distinction in so disreputable a profession as Law. Any intelligent opponent of Hamilton's nationalist views ought to be glad this man's still amang us. Another Scot with life and wit to him is Alastair Hetherington, whose *Inside BBC Scotland 1975-1980* (Whitewater Press) is an interesting memoir of rather more that went on in the country in those years.

Saunders Lewis was dubbed "my Welsh counterpart" by MacDiarmid and this rightish

RC francophile's brief *verse oeuvre* in new versions tr. J.P. Clancy is most welcome, *Selected Poems*, from the University of Wales Press, who also do a *Selected Works of David Jones* ed. John Matthias, and *Wales in His Arms*, Dylan Thomas's selection of Welsh poetry. Gwyn Williams' *Introduction to Welsh Literature* is also commended. The earliest Welsh poems were written in Scotland as our reviewer of a literary history long ago noted!

John Byrne's play *Colquhoun and Mac-Bryde*, Faber, £4.99, finds here a cataloguist scunnered to death with gossip about artists. I shall continue to revere the paintings of Robert Colquhoun and MacBrydes and swear to ignore any play on the life of John Byrne! That said, the banter between B & C at times reaches *Slab Boys* standards, but Byrne seems less interested in literary London (can you blame him?), and the pace drops noticeably whenever anybody else drops by.

Edinburgh University Press's Modern Scottish Writers series now reaches *Liz Lochhead's Voices* ed. Crawford and Varty, £14.95. The volume is slimmer than it should be, but a real attempt is made to match the criticism to the style and tone of the work itself. As regards the new renaissance in Scottish Literary Culture referred to in the same publisher's *The Scottish Novel since the Seventies*, one would probably be trampled to death by those who'd deny the renaissance was mostly quantitative. Somebody ought to say that, even if it isn't true. Anette Degott-Reinhardt's *Norman MacCaigs Lyrisches Werk*, Peter Lang / Scottish Studies Centre, DM89, is in German and thorough as a study. Its analysis, unfortunately, tends towards the superficial, and MacCaig's mischievous irony is imperfectly comprehended. There's a review in which MacCaig speaks more nonsense about philosophy than anyone without an academic post in it has the right to. (He'd be the first to enjoy the joke!) Not the first publication by this author on this theme is Colin Manlove's *Scottish Fantasy Literature*, from Hogg, J, to Elphinstone, M, Canongate. Then RLS: *Robert Louis Stevenson & France* by Louis Stott, Creag Darach Publications, Milton of Aberfoyle FK8 3TD, looks bitty, has photos, but contains much information, not tidily, but accessibly set down. *The Ring of Words* pinches an RLS phrase to entitle a pamphlet, £2.99, same author and publisher, on literary landmarks of Stirling and Clackmannan.

Joanna Russ's *How to Suppress Women's Writing* (The Women's Press) might be referred to a psychologist as a useful special study of general pathological psychological devices at work in such exclusions as operate well beyond the specific ambit the title points to. £6.99, like their *The Fires of Bride*, a fantasy of some Scottish isle in which *fay comme tu voudras* has been the author, Ellen Galford's, watchword. Rich and taudry pickings, a mischievous spirit at work if ever I saw it, if, I say modestly, a little rich for the contents of *my* tartan weskit, but that's my problem, not hers. *Black Diamonds and the Blue Brazil*, Northern Books/ Famedram, is about coal-mining Cowdenbeath's fitba team and might identify a venue for future surrealist fancy.

More topical than it might seem to some, *In the Service of Life* by Leah Leneman, Mercat, the story of Elsie Inglis and the Scottish women's hospitals asks questions to put a lot of not-dead issues into focus. The autobiography of Mary Morton Hardie, *A Cinder Glows*, Eric Dobby Publishing, Orpington, Kent, £12.99, is not so much a Dickensian story as a piece of concise naturalism better informed than much social fiction, and puslating with that *Ancient Mariner's* compulsion to tell you a bloody good story. Canongate's Flashbacks series includes *Two Generations of Edinburgh Folk*, and *Hard Work, ye ken* on Midlothian women farmworkers, reminiscences in honest language. The same publisher's *More Frost and Snow*, ed. Mowbray Pearson, is the diary of Janet Burnet from 1758-95, a contribution to the Sources in Local History series.

Canty and Couthie ed Anne Forsyth, is poems Rorie and Murray, TS Cairncross et al., from Aberdeen's Scottish Cultural Press, £5.95, which sells Douglas Kynoch's *Teach yourself Doric* at £4.95, and with astonishing energy and commitment, promises to revolutionarise the Scottish publishing scene with the same radical zeal as we ourselves aspire to. Gordon Jarvie's *The Scottish Reciter*, The Black Staff Press (Belfast) is a good bargain from Lord Ullin til Oor Hamlet, superior of its kind. Book Trust Scotland's *Off The Shelf* is a guide to Scotland's writers and illustrators for children, and a very efficient job.

Notes on Contributors

W P Anderson:has spent several of the last 15 years overseas. Now home, he's received Canada Council funding to work on a novel, *Acts of Faith.*

Sheena Blackhall: poet, short story writer, illustrator, single parent and psychology student. New poetry collection, *Druids, Drachts, Drochles,* due out this year.

Rosalind Brackenbury writes fiction and poetry. Latest work is *Going Home The Long Way Round The Mountain* (Taxus Press,1993)

Colin Donald is a freelance jounalist and a regular contributor to *The Scotsman.*

Gavin Ewart: b London, 1916. His latest book (1993) is *85 Poems* (Hutchinson).

Tom Flannagan has won many composition and story telling competitions.

Iain Galbraith: b Glasgow. Has translated criticism, fiction and poetry from German. Poetry and short prose in various magazines.

Rob Griffith: singer, songwriter, living in Stirling. Tape, *Firth and Mountain,* released in 1991. Has won the Edinburgh Folk Club song-writing competition.

Sandy Harvey works in community care in Falkirk. Her other main interest is Scottish fiddle music and art.

Tom Hubbard: ex librarian and lecturer. Books: *Four Fife Poets*; *The New Makars*; *Seeking Mr Hyde.* Currently writing a novel about the painter Marie Bashkirtseff.

Jessie Kesson: b Inverness 1916, died September 1995. Lived in London for 45 years. Three novels (two became prize winning films), collection of short stories, several plays for radio and TV.

Frank Kuppner: Next book, *Life on a Dead Planet,* is due out from Polygon in late 1993.

Lorn Macintyre: Many poems and short stories published; three novels in Chronicle of Invernevis series; fourth, *The Waterloo Woods in Retreat,* completed.

Alastair Mackie: Aberdonian poet, translator and retired teacher. Graduated in English 1950 Aberdeen University. Took to Scots 1954.

Maureen Macnaughtan: Co-founder of the Moray and Nairn Writers' Workshop. Her poetry has been widely published.

Hugh MacPherson: b Scotland, 1953. Has published poems, stories and articles.

Linda McCann runs Maryhill Women Writers Group, and has edited an anthology of their work, *The Cat's Mother.* Has been writer in residence in Glasgow.

Gordon Meade is Writing Fellow and writer in residence in Dundee. Second collection, *The Scrimshaw Sailor,* forthcoming with Chapman publications.

Mary Montgomery: Born 1955, in Lewis. Poetry widely puboished in Scotland and Ireland. Her novel, Clann Iseabail is to be published by Acair.

George Pryde: Stress Engineer, b. Glasgow 1934. Short stories in various magazines and anthologies. First novel completed.

Salvatore Quasimodo (1901-68): Poet, translator, critic. Nobel Prize winner 1959. Early preoccupation with classical forms changes with war experience to a commitment to Italy's suffering under Nazis (1943-46).

Mario Relich is a contributor to the *Larousse Dictionary of Writers.*

Peter Snow teaches drama and English at the Edinburgh Rudolf Steiner School.

Isobel Grant Stewart lives in Alloa and is a freelance writer. Poems in Arts Council Anthology (1952) and in several *Macgregors' Gathering* Anthologies (BBC publications).

Bill Turner: poet, novelist, creative writing tutor, radio playwright, and reviewer. Now a pensioner, but not burnt out yet...

Brian Whittingham: first poetry collection *Ergonomic Workstations & Spinning tea-cans* (Taranis Books, 1992); creative writing tutor; on the editorial board of *WestCoast* magazine.

Christopher Whyte: teaches Scottish Literature in Glasgow. Editing a book on gender and sexualities in modern Scottish literature, *Gendering the Nation* (EUP, 1995)